the
focused life

the
focused life

and other devotions for church groups

edward l. hayes

 **BAKER BOOK HOUSE**
Grand Rapids, Michigan 49506

PHOTOLITHOPRINTED BY CUSHING - MALLOY, INC.
ANN ARBOR, MICHIGAN, UNITED STATES OF AMERICA

Contents

Preface

The meaning of life is to build a life as if it were a work of art. People are interested in knowing how to live life better and well. In their quest, they find that the Bible holds fundamental answers. The insights and wisdom that flow from the pages of Scripture touch universally common experiences. Christ calls us to experience common things in life in uncommon manner.

These essays on the Christian experience have emerged out of years of reflection on my own Christian faith. The lives of others, my own family included, have added an immeasurable dimension to my Christian life. My aim in writing these essays is to help the reader recover something of the meaning of the transcendent life. The use of the Scriptures is primary throughout. When reference is made to contemporary literature, classics from history, and quotations from great minds, the purpose is never to detract from God's revealed truth. Rather, it is meant to illustrate that truth and lend further credence to the Christian message.

Years of dialogue with theological students, church leaders, and common people have led me to conclude what others have discovered. We all want to change institutions and other people, but few of us want to follow the Spirit's call for our own inner renewal.

1
The Focused Life

There is power in determining a central focus to life. Jesus invites us to "seek first his kingdom and his righteousness" (Matt. 6:33) and Paul urged Christians to "set your mind on the things above" (Col. 3:2, NASB). In his rebuke of Peter, Jesus charged that he did not set his mind on God's interest, but man's (Matt. 16:23). The agenda for the Christian must always be to place the things of God first above all else. Life with a single focus on God has a habit of falling into place, all parts having meaning and potentially reaping contentment and great reward.

Life's tragedies can be blunted by a life of singular purpose. Fanny Crosby, the famous blind hymn writer, created song out of sorrow and blessing out of blindness, and generations have been touched by her triumphs. We too can face every trial with a godly perspective born of reflection on the Scriptures. "Consider it all joy," James instructs us, "when you encounter various trials" (James 1:2, NASB

God's answer to the barrenness of business is a single focus. Bonhoeffer, in *Life Together*, writes of the significance of beginning the day with God. "The prayer of the morning," he observed, "will determine the day." Issues of the soul take precedence over the mad scramble to acquire things, to expand wealth and influence; they take precedence over aimless activism as well. When the inner spirit is renewed, the outer man is also restored. Despite the stresses of a busy life, Paul could claim that "the inward man is renewed day by day" (2 Cor. 4:16, KJV).

It was said of John Knox that the voice of that one man did more to inspire people to action than ten thousand trumpets blustering in people's ears. His secret was the focused life. As a reformation leader, no uncertain sound came from his lips. Yet even common folk can influence many by a Spirit-filled life.

The issue is one of focus and filling. Tozer's *Pursuit of God* has inspired many to seek God. Tournier's *Person Reborn* and Trueblood's *Incendiary Fellowship* continue to light the fires of faith in one direction—fulfilling the deep quest of the human heart to focus life on God above all else.

We must look to Jesus, the author and perfecter of our faith (Heb. 12:2). He alone points the way to God and provides the road map for time and eternity. Jesus is the Great Shepherd of the soul. Without him as both guide and goal we remain adrift, aimless wanderers through life.

Years ago, the Dutch Reformation leader Erasmus wrote, "By a Carpenter mankind was made and only by a Carpenter can mankind be remade." Life reshaped to conform to the attractive image of Christ will provide both a compass and a magnet—a compass to show us the path of godliness and a magnet to attract others to the Savior.

2

The Powerful Life

Our world is obsessed with power. An awesome struggle exists between nations over who will be number one in world influence. The arms race continues despite peace conferences. Kingpins of power use their ploys to gain a favorable edge, if only for a day.

Richard Halverson, chaplain of the U.S. Senate, senses a growing frustration in Washington. He describes how the most powerful government on earth cannot solve problems. "What becomes evident is the clear inadequacy of human legislation to change human nature." This same concern was expressed by Arthur Schlesinger, Jr., in *Crisis of Confidence*. "How can we solve the panic of our souls?" he asked.

In the midst of this crisis the message of the gospel and the power of the cross seem pitifully weak. Yet this authority outclasses every power center known to man.

World history is one long testimony to Lord Acton's maxim, "Power tends to corrupt and absolute power corrupts absolutely." When Jesus invaded our history he demonstrated a power to save rather than destroy. This divine show of force was not with military or political influence. Rather than being corrupt, it brought healing.

Jesus claimed power as a personal possession shared by the Father. It was a property of his very being. Such a dramatic display of authority and power through word and miracle stunned his enemies and sparked a revolution. His power didn't put people down. It turned people's hearts toward God.

The miracles of Jesus were never magical or staged. They flowed from his divine compassion and touched the genuine ills and hurts of a sin-ridden world. Our world became inflamed with the passionate power of a loving Savior. This power is shared with us. Jesus said: "All power is given unto me in heaven and in earth.... I am with you alway" (Matt. 28:18, 20, KJV). We must take our cue from Christ. Any act of caring, any obedient service must be prompted by genuine compassion. Words alone will not do. "The Kingdom of God is not a matter of talk but of power" (1 Cor. 4:20). Above all, our caring must issue from the power source of Christ himself.

The Bible speaks of this power in a variety of ways. By it the world was formed, Israel was delivered, history was shaped, all things hold together, and salvation has come. Isaiah declared: "He is strong in power" (Isa. 40:26, RSV). God as Creator and Preserver of the world creates and upholds it by the word of his power. "God is our refuge and strength," sang the psalmist (Ps. 46:1, RSV). Also, the great doxologies of Scripture laud the power of God. These are not empty sentimentalities. They fairly glow with passion and confidence in a strong God.

In the New Testament God's power is revealed in his Son and his Holy Spirit. The Messiah of Israel was peculiarly a manifestation of the power of God. God-in-residence was power on display. Exampled by miracle, it was supremely shown by the resurrection of Jesus from the dead. At Pentecost it sparked a spreading flame.

Power cannot be purchased. Simon Magus discovered this. Known as "the great power of God" (Acts 8:10, KJV) to superstitious first-century citizens, this man's power dimmed alongside the genuine thing. Offering to buy Holy Spirit power, Simon Magus was rebuked by Peter. His name is now only a dictionary entry under *simony,* the crime of buying or selling religious favor.

The powerful life is a productive life. All of God's power is directed toward man's ultimate good. That must be our pattern also. The mere existence of spiritual gifts in the church is the result of shared power.

The powerful life is a confronting life. We are engaged in cosmic battle with the powers of darkness. "Greater is he that is in you, than he that is in the world" (1 John 4:4, KJV). The power of the indwelling Christ is adequate to resist satanic attack and temptation to evil. Such power is rarely used in our indulgent society.

Above all, the powerful life holds out the tantalizing possibility of demonstrating Christian love. "Love one another" is no hollow command. In Christ it becomes a reality. In the summer of 1972 when Sargent Shriver accepted the democratic nomination for vice president, he quoted Pierre Teilhard de Chardin: "Someday, after we have mastered the winds, the waves, the tides, and gravity, we will harness for God the energies of love: and then for the second time in the history of the world man will have discovered fire."

3
The Contented Life

Contentment is a rare commodity these days. Many people seek it; few find it. Our age is characterized by a frantic search for personal happiness. There are some who even claim it as a divine right. Like those Christians who salute success as the inherent right of the faithful, people who seek satisfaction as a goal have a twisted theology and warped view of the Christian experience. Contentment is something gained—not something pursued. Its peaceful dimensions are described in the Scriptures.

Contentment is delight in God—not in possessions. Jesus warned, "Watch out! Be on your guard against all kinds of greed; a man's life does not consist in the abundance of his possessions" (Luke 12:15). Someone has defined contentment as wanting few things. Our Lord wisely spoke of being "rich toward God" (Luke 12:21), and David advised, "Delight yourself in the Lord and he will give you the desires of your heart" (Ps. 37:4).

Contentment, furthermore, is mastery of circumstances—not withdrawal from the struggles of life. The Bible is the story of the weak who learned to use God's power. God does not invite us to retreat to caves for contemplation, but to advance in faith and confront the enemy of our souls. In the struggle we are given assurance of overcoming through faith: "Thanks be to God, who always leads us in triumphal procession in Christ..." (2 Cor. 2:14). The rocky places in life are only stepping stones to God's grace. The Scriptures instruct us to be strong in the Lord and in his mighty power (Eph. 6:10).

The contented life is also the happy life described by Jesus in the Sermon on the Mount (Matt. 5:3–10). In the Beatitudes Jesus points out that contentment is possessed by the poor in spirit, those who mourn, the meek, the spiritually hungry, the merciful, the pure in heart, the peacemakers, and the persecuted. Stack this up against the futile search for happiness by many of our contemporaries. In *The Taste of Joy* Calvin Miller writes that there is "nothing more barren than the pursuit of happiness."

Contentment does not come on fancy platters served up on banquet tables. Rather, it is a quality of life gained through serving others. I have yet to meet a Christian whose life of selfless service has produced anything other than some sense of contentment. On the other hand, I have met bitter, cynical, and fearful people whose goals of fulfillment have not been attained.

In the David Livingston museum near Glasgow there stands a stained-glass window given by the United Free Church of Scotland in 1932. Its inscription is taken from the pioneer missionary's diary. It reads, simply: "I will place no value on anything I have or possess, except in relation to the kingdom of Christ."

4
The Seeking Life

Every life is a profession of some kind of faith and exercises an inevitable and silent propaganda. It influences either for good or evil. Whatever we seek first sets the course and destiny of our lives. When Jesus Christ is at the center of our lives, the very fragrance of Christ exudes from us and our world is much the better for it.

Consciously or unconsciously, all of us give ourselves to some one allegiance. As life moves on, some one motive (or group of motives) grows stronger until there is captivity to some one obedience.

There are many possible goals in life, but not all lead to peace, contentment, and personal fulfillment. The passion for possessions is one such false goal. "Theirs is an endless road, a hopeless maze," wrote Bernard of Clairvaux, "who seek goods before they seek God." This is what Paul meant when he commanded Christians to keep seeking the things above where Christ is seated at the right hand of God (Col. 3:1). That is to say, our loyalties and the bent of our lives should be directed to God above all else.

Solomon advised Hebrew sons to seek wisdom. "Make your ear attentive to wisdom," he wrote. "Incline your heart to understanding" (Prov. 2:2,

NASB). The wisest man who ever lived further advised: "If you seek her as silver, and search for her as for hidden treasures; then you will discern the fear of the LORD, and discover the knowledge of God" (Prov. 2:4, 5, NASB). If we are lacking wisdom, instructs James, we are to ask for it (1:5). And when it is found, we will discover that wisdom from above is pure, peaceable, gentle, reasonable, full of mercy and good fruits, unwavering, and without hypocrisy (James 3:17).

Jesus taught that no one can serve two masters (Matt. 6:24). We must decide between the two. For a while the human will may be poised between one or the other, but ultimately the scale is tipped. One service or the other must be chosen. In the same way, James advised, "A double minded man is unstable in all his ways" (1:8, KJV).

Jesus also taught that we are to seek first the kingdom of God and his righteousness (Matt. 6:33). The words of Christ are compelling and convincing. We are to direct our thoughts and our actions both steadily and continually toward the will and the glory of God. All of life's priorities, options, and choices fade in their significance when placed in divine perspective.

Peace is to be pursued in our world (Heb. 12:14). "Seek peace and pursue it," cried the psalmist David (Ps. 34:14). Peace is no idyllic fantasy conjured up in the minds of the weak and fainthearted. It arises from the nature of God himself, it was incarnated in the Prince of Peace, and it is one of the fruits of the Spirit. Peace reflects not only the dimension of healing and wholeness made possible by the blood of Christ, but also it shines upon all human relationships when Christ who is our Peace rules in each life.

Above all else, we are to seek the Lord while he may be found. "Seek Me that you may live," thundered the message of the prophet Amos to the people of the eighth century B.C. "Those who come to God," write the author of Hebrews, "must believe that he is, and that He is a rewarder of those who seek Him" (Heb. 11:6, NASB). Johann Frank expressed it well in his German hymn, *Jesu, Meine Freude.*

> Jesus priceless treasure,
> Source of purest pleasure,
> Truest friend to me;
> Long my heart hath panted,
> 'Til it well nigh fainted,
> Thirsting after thee,
> Thine I am, O spotless Lamb,
> I will suffer naught to hide thee,
> Ask for naught beside thee.

J. I. Packer once made an insightful analysis of our generation: "We have conformed to the modern spirit: the spirit, that is, that spawns great thoughts of man and leaves room for only small thoughts of God." The seeking life, quite the opposite of the spirit of the age, enlarges our minds and expands our God-consciousness. "O God, thou art my God," we are to pray. "Early will I seek thee" (Ps. 63:1, KJV).

5
The Peaceful Life

Jesus was on the side of peace. "Blessed are the peacemakers," he said, "for they shall be called sons of God" (Matt. 5:9, NASB). The Prince of Peace had a singular mission in his incarnation: peace. But his goal was not merely to reconcile cosmic disorder (the result of estrangement between God and man through the fall of Adam); his coming brought healing to our marred humanity and wholeness to our relationships. As children of his kingdom we are to pursue peace with all (Heb. 12:14).

Thomas à Kempis advised Christians: "Keep yourself first in peace, and then you shall be able to pacify others." Personal serenity, a goal of every ancient Greek stoic, never found its source until Jesus came. Peace is not merely the absence of war or conflict. It is the abiding presence of Christ.

A peaceful person does more good than a learned man. "Who is wise and understanding among you?" asked James. "By his good life let him show his works in the meekness of wisdom" (3:13, RSV). The truly wise person displays heavenly wisdom which the Bible describes as first pure, then peaceable (James 3:17). Peace, we are told, surpasses all understanding (Phil. 4:7).

The secret of inner peace is divine forgiveness. Those at war with one another do not know the language of forgiveness. Reconciliation is foreign to them—a sign of weakness. Jesus made peace through the blood of his cross (Col. 1:20). This dominant theme of apostolic preaching is also the heart of the gospel and the heritage of every Christian. "Let the peace of Christ rule in your hearts," Paul urged first-century Christians (Col. 3:15).

Peace is the gift of the Father and the Son obtained and maintained through communion with Christ. Martin Luther, the sixteenth-century reformer, discovered this fundamental truth after years of agonizing penance. Unable to soothe the inner anguish of his soul, Luther finally found solace in Christ. As a professor of Holy Scripture at Wittenberg, he discovered the liberating truth of Romans 5:1: "Therefore, since we are justified by faith, we have peace with God." The reality of Peter's benediction became Luther's personal possession: "Peace to all of you who are in Christ" (1 Peter 5:14).

The peace Jesus gives differs substantially from that of the world. "My peace I give unto you," Jesus said; "Not as the world giveth, give I unto you" (John 14:27, kjv). The current peace movement suffers from failure to realize that peace is more than the absence of conflict. Our world's agenda for peace will never be met until there is a recognition that peace begins within the human soul. Jesus pointed out the fallacy of misplaced faith in peace. There can be no lasting peace without salvation from sin.

The peace Jesus gives also divides people. "Do not think," the Master taught, "that I have come to bring peace on earth; I have not come to bring peace, but a sword" (Matt. 10:34, RSV). Who has not puzzled over these strong words? They seem to contradict the angelic message announcing his birth and the very nature of God himself. Whatever their mystery, these words of the Messiah indicate the illusiveness of peace. There is no easy peace, no romantic utopianism in his kingdom. The good news of the gospel is also accompanied by the bad news of man's sinfulness. Repentance, reconciliation, and divine forgiveness are the platforms of a genuine peace movement.

Yet we are urged to be peacemakers in our world. Christians are not exempt from this responsibility during these tragic times. If peacemakers are the true children of God, as Jesus taught in the beatitude, then we must work with all our might to pursue peace. The Bible commands it: "So then let us pursue the things which make for peace" (Rom. 14:19, NASB). How can we impact our society with the biblical perspective of life abundant as well as life eternal? The peace message of the gospel must also be the peace mission of the faithful. Placing peace solely in a heavenly framework is a form of escapism and is intolerably inconsistent with Christianity.

It is easy to withdraw and become cynical. How can my efforts effect peace on earth? Why not sit it out and wait for the coming kingdom of peace? Cynics are only too happy to make the world as barren to others as it is to themselves. Christians, on the contrary, are not cynics. They are optimists. While lasting peace may never be an earthly reality, as emissaries of salt and light we are called to a high mission.

"How beautiful are the feet of those
Who preach the Gospel of peace with God
And bring glad tidings of good things."
(Rom. 10:15, LB).

6
The Faithful Life

Our world suffers from an inadequate view of God. As a result, we have an inadequate view of life. Defining God in human terms leads to pessimism, skepticism, and alienation. The idea of a faithful God seems absurd. Yet that is how the Bible reveals him.

For many people, the existence of God is not a question; he isn't even in their thoughts. When the notion does cross their mind, they are apt to lash out against him, as did the famous historian H. G. Wells. Viewing the troubles and trials of life he concluded: "God is an ever absent help in time of trouble."

The only predictable thing about life is its unpredictability. Not so with God. The Scripture reveals him as the Faithful One. "It is God alone from whom we receive all good," wrote Martin Luther, "and by whom we are delivered from all evil." The reformer's students once asked what it meant to have a God. Luther's wise reply should give comfort and hope to all of us: "A god is that from which we are to expect everything good and to which we are to take refuge in all times of need."

Such simplicity is hard for moderns to swallow. Our problem is that we tend to make God in our own image, forgetting that it happened the other way around.

Ancient Job had a larger-than-life view of God. Such a faith gave him strength to endure excruciating suffering. Despite all that plagued him Job confessed, "You gave me life and showed me kindness, and in your providence watched over my spirit" (Job 10:12). Told by his wife to curse God and die, Job did not sin nor charge God foolishly. "Though he slay me," Job declared, "yet will I hope in him" (Job 13:15, NIV).

An adequate view of God also helped ease Jeremiah's crushing burdens. Oppressed, abandoned, and rejected, he failed to lose faith in God or place blame on him for his troubles. By his own admission he was a man "who has seen affliction" (Lam. 3:1). Yet he affirmed, "Because of the Lord's great love we are not consumed, for his compassions never fail. They are new every morning; great is your faithfulness" (Lam. 3:22–23).

For Paul it was a shipwreck that tried his faith: "Keep up your courage, men, for I have faith in God that it will happen just as he told me" (Acts 27:25). To the Corinthians he confessed directly and simply, "God is faithful" (1 Cor. 1:9, KJV).

The faithfulness of God is revealed through power to forgive. "He is faithful and just, and will forgive our sins," wrote John the apostle (1 John 1:9, RSV). When wronged by others, we find it terribly difficult to be forgiving. But not God. Calvary and its cross made forgiveness possible.

The faithfulness of God is also evidenced by God's promises. "He will never leave you nor forsake you," wrote Moses (Deut. 31:6). When abandoned, betrayed, or forsaken by others, we cannot help but experience terrible disappointment and a sense of loss. God is not like that. His word can be trusted.

The faithfulness of God is painted boldly on the canvas of his creation. God's love, goodness, and mercy touch us all. His total reliability stands out in stark contrast to our own failures and unfaithfulness. God's faithful character has broken in on us to set a standard for us to follow. We love God, wrote John the apostle, because he first loved us (1 John 4:19). That kind of love comes from a faithful God.

7
The Steady Life

People tend to admire a person whose goals in life are unmistakably clear. Those who possess calm and cool certainty are looked up to and often followed. Most of us, however, are destined to unsteady lives. But Christ invites us to steadiness, living lives founded on faith, persevering to the end.

Jesus, who specialized in lifting the discouraged, healing the broken, and rescuing the lost, placed a high value on the steady life. Nowhere in his teachings is the steady life more central than in his words, "No one who puts his hand to the plow and looks back is fit for...the kingdom of God" (Luke 9:62).

The inner certainty we all crave is rooted in a firm faith in God. Our living is to be patterned after the One who said, "I am the Lord, I change not" (Mal. 3:6, KJV). Just as a navigator fixes a sextant to a star, so the Christian looks to Jesus as the author and perfecter of faith (Heb. 12:2). When God sets the compass, the steady life is a reality.

This kind of life is not to be confused with an easy life. "A thousand trials surround those who live by faith," commented Chiang Kai-shek shortly before his death. Trouble is at every corner. Job knew this and wrote, "Man is born unto trouble, as the sparks fly upward" (Job 5:7, KJV). Life will have its ups and downs but Jesus steadies the ship.

Those who experience rough seas and rocky paths will find that God is totally adequate. Corrie ten Boom, whose faith in God saw her through terrifying times in a Nazi concentration camp during World War II, was able to write, "No pit is so deep that He is not deeper still."

The steady life is a life of high purpose and even higher trust. After viewing the seeming emptiness and meaninglessness of life, Solomon concluded: "Fear God and keep his commandments, for this is the whole duty of man" (Eccles. 12:13). Centuries later the prophet Micah stated the same truth: "And what does the Lord require of you? To act justly and to love mercy and to walk humbly with your God" (Mic. 6:8).

The steady life carries more than its share of hope. "We have this hope as an anchor for the soul," writes the author of Hebrews (Heb. 6:19). Like an anchor in a storm, hope steadies the soul. The reality of Christian hope is the resurrection of Christ from the dead. This fact of history opens the door to eternity. It transforms our mortality to immortality.

The steady life is the persevering life. This is no "grin and bear it" kind of thing. We are not called to become like the ancient Greek stoics who believed that any show of emotion diminished the power of their gods. Rather, we are to develop patience through trials. Faith and hope are not escape mechanisms or parachutes for bailing out when life becomes difficult. They are the fiber that makes us strong while experiencing tough times. "You need to persevere so that when you have done the will of God, you will receive what he has promised" (Heb. 10:36).

Based on a solid foundation of faith and motivated by hope, the steady life is fired by fresh new vigor to face life's demands. "They that wait upon the Lord shall renew their strength," proclaimed Isaiah. "They shall mount up with wings as eagles; they shall run, and not be weary; and they shall walk, and not faint" (Isa. 40:31, KJV). "Stand firm," urged Paul to first-century Corinthian Christians; "let nothing move you" (1 Cor. 15:58).

Day after day Christopher Columbus entered these words in the log of the Santa Maria: "This day we sailed on." That might make a good motto for the steady life.

8
The Forgiving Life

God forgives and forgets. This divine capacity is part of his nature. Unfortunately, it doesn't come naturally for us humans. Do something right and the world ignores you. Do something wrong and they never let you forget it.

Contrary to common opinion, the Bible does not paint a picture of a doting God who tolerates sin like a permissive parent. Quite the opposite, he deals in grace with repentant people. God's grace is on display because of the judgment Jesus bore for our sake. God doesn't overlook sin, but he does forgive sinners and remembers their sins no more (Ps. 103:12).

While forgiveness is the free and gracious act of a loving God, it is also an activity for human beings to engage in. Jesus taught his disciples to pray, "Forgive us our debts, as we forgive our debtors" (Matt. 6:12, KJV). Forgiveness is the true badge of the new life in Christ. "Just as the Lord forgave you," Paul explained to Colossian Christians, "so also should you" be "forgiving each other" (Col. 3:13, NASB).

Devote yourself thoroughly to forgiving others. In so doing you might right a wrong and restore a wrongdoer. We are to forgive no matter what response we get from the other person. Forgiving starts with a free choice. It is ours to make.

Develop the fine art of forgetting petty wrongs and unkind acts. "Be kind to one another, tender-hearted, forgiving each other," Paul urged the Christians at Ephesus (4:32, NASB). A friend of Clara Barton, founder of the American Red Cross, once reminded Clara of an especially cruel thing done to her years before. "Don't you remember it?" her friend asked. "No," came the reply, "but I do distinctly remember forgetting it."

No one can be free and happy by harboring grudges. "Seek peace and pursue it" is good advice. Long before modern psychology determined that unresolved anger has the potential of making one physically ill, the Bible offered healthy words: "See to it ... that no root of bitterness springing up causes trouble" (Heb. 12:15, NASB).

Leave all vengeance up to God. "Don't repay evil for evil," counseled Paul (1 Peter 3:9, LB). To do so is to make anger our master. When we are incapable of controlling our own spirit we are, as the proverb says, "a city that is broken down, and without walls" (Prov. 25:28, KJV).

We also need to forgive ourselves. We are often harder on ourselves than on others. To err is human; God is aware of our weaknesses. Since God removes our sins (when they are confessed) as far as the east is from the west (Ps. 103:12) we should no longer hold past mistakes against ourselves.

The forgiving life is a realistic life. It takes into account the fruit of our actions and attitudes. Life lived humbly before God and others results in goodwill, peace of mind, and contentment of soul. Life lived bitterly toward enemies returns a harvest of ill will, animosity, and strife. A man once commented to John Wesley, the founder of Methodism, "I never forgive." Wesley replied, "Then sir, I hope that you never sin."

The forgiving life is a costly life. Jesus said we are to forgive not merely once but seventy times seven. This is outrageously difficult. It is easier to pass off another's fault or abrasive insult by saying, "It doesn't matter." Ignoring an offender, however, fails to fulfill the requirement to forgive. To all those who harbor bitterness, who gloss over sin, who fail to forgive, these penetrating words of Jesus speak all too clearly: "But if you do not forgive men their sins, your Father will not forgive your sins" (Matt. 6:15).

Experience the relief and release of forgiveness. Live to forgive. That is the way of Christ.

9
The Adequate Life

The Christian life is an adequate life. Faith in God gives fundamental answers to life's big questions. "For to me, to live is Christ," wrote Paul to first-century Philippian believers, "and to die is gain" (Phil. 1:21). Such a distillation of wisdom is shared by few, yet available through faith in Jesus Christ.

During the Second World War the troop ship *Dorchester* went down off the coast of England. The story of how the four chaplains aboard gave their lifejackets to sailors and soldiers is now a national legend. They were last seen linked arm in arm with each other, praying as the ship sank. In 1974 this incredible act of faith and bravery was memorialized in a commemorative United States postal stamp. But the real story didn't end in a brave act.

Protestant chaplain Clark V. Poling wrote his parents just before the ill-fated voyage. "Pray for me. Pray not that I will be safe. War is never safe. Pray only that I will be an adequate man." That letter and the faith of Chaplain Poling have inspired many.

The adequate life is a life of faith. Its calm, certain style flows from life in unity with God. Faith is more than a crutch in time of trouble. It is

33

a habit of life. Without faith it is impossible to please God, states the maxim from Hebrews. "For he who comes to God must believe that he is, and that He is a rewarder of those who seek Him" (Heb. 11:6, NASB). We are to walk by faith and not by sight.

This is not easy for us. We would rather be self-possessed, self-assured, confident people needing no outside help. Faith, so the Bible teaches, "is the assurance of things hoped for, the conviction of things not seen" (Heb. 11:1, NASB).

The life of faith is one that is centered in Christ, rooted in the Scriptures, and led by the Spirit. What more could we ask?

There is more to the adequate life than meets the eye. It is also marked by hope. While mortality is our middle name, there is life after death. As a ship is safe with an anchor, so a Christian is secured by hope. Peter told oppressed refugees of first-century persecution that they were "born anew to a living hope through the resurrection of Jesus Christ from the dead" (1 Peter 1:3, RSV).

Hope puts song in our heart and spring in our walk, and it gives us courage to face tomorrow. A life lived with the sterling quality of hope prompts others to ask the reason for it. When God is sanctified in the heart, when there is readiness to give an answer, and when that answer is given in meekness and with reverence for God, despairing people discover the hope of the gospel (1 Peter 3:15).

No life is complete without love. Extolled by prophets, exhibited uniquely by Jesus, and exhorted by the apostles, love is the highest virtue. The entire law of God is summed up in it. It is love that models the grace of God to our watching world. Sign and proof of faith, mark of true discipleship, and the only motive for evangelism and true service toward others, love is all that really endures.

The adequate life, then, balances out the triad of virtues found repeatedly in the Bible—faith, hope, and love. Its rich display of integrity knows no match among the phony, plastic lifestyles of our contemporaries. Ultimately its attractive quality serves as a magnet toward others.

Oswald Chambers, whose timeless writings explored the wellspring of Christ, wrote helpful words to all who feel inadequate. "Keep right at the Source," he said, "and out of you will flow rivers of living life, irrepressible life."

10
The Lonely Life

Loneliness is one of the maladies of our time. Anyone who has experienced the crushing depression that comes with estrangement, divorce, or any great loss, can testify to its terror. Being alone, the feeling of being unwanted, and the lack of close friends are the worst kind of poverty, one that most of us have experienced at one time or another.

The Bible tells of real people who bore the ache of loneliness. Moses objected to God, "I am not able to carry all this people alone" (Num. 11:14, RSV). In his distress David cried out, "No man cares for me" (Ps. 142:4, RSV). Elijah, hiding in a cave, concluded, "I, even I only, am left" (1 Kings 19:10, RSV). Even Jesus was left alone to face his tormenters. Matthew recorded the pathetic cowardice of the disciples and the loneliness of the Master in Gethsemane: "Then all the disciples forsook him and fled" (Matt. 26:56, RSV).

Helplessness and abandonment test the fiber of faith. One can never fully know whether or not one's faith will prove strong enough until put to the test of loneliness. This is where Christianity is at its best. For Paul to understand fully God's declaration that "My grace is sufficient" (2 Cor. 12:9, RSV) he had to experience the loss of all things. David and Job and a host of prophets affirmed this truth in their own loneliness. "Thou art my refuge" (Ps. 142:5, RSV), declared David, and despite wrenching pain and loss, Job affirmed, "Thy care has preserved my spirit" (Job 10:12, RSV).

The mastery of loneliness is one of life's great goals. In this task we are not left to our own devices. At rock bottom is the foundational truth of God's presence: "I will never leave thee, nor forsake thee" (Heb. 13:5, KJV). Here is the promise of God himself, given first to Moses and repeated in the New Testament.

The presence of God is more than hollow words. The only adequate antidote to loneliness is trust and faith in a God who is close at all times. David's classic Psalm 23 frames a peaceful scene of a shepherd leading sheep by quiet waters in green pastures. But life consists of more than bubbling brooks. Turbulence is never far away. "Even though I walk through the valley of the shadow of death," David wrote, "I will fear no evil, for you are with me" (Ps. 23:4).

In the dark night of our loneliness, God is there. "I lie awake," cried the psalmist. "I have become like a bird alone on a housetop" (Ps. 102:7). Our tendency is to distance ourselves from God. Yet he never moves. His absolute and unfailing love unlocks the prison door of our loneliness.

Out of the distant past of my own childhood comes the memory of a gospel song sung often in our little church: "No longer lonely, no longer lonely, for Jesus is a friend of friends to me." It is the

Spirit who helps our weakness. To be Christ's is to possess a friend who sticks closer than a brother. It is enough to know that in the lonely life Jesus is there.

11
The Spirit-filled Life

God's call to freedom is the appeal, "Be filled with the Spirit." There is no more misdirected a life than a self-directed life. Filling up one's existence with an orientation toward the Creator assures harmony, peace, joy, and true freedom. When we elevate our own egos and become self-centered we leave little room for the Spirit.

It is God's Spirit who settles our doubts, quells our suspicions, and opens our hearts to the life of freedom in the gospel. Those born of the Spirit experience eternal life—exuberant, joy-filled life.

God calls us to productive, useful living. That is why he places his Spirit within us by faith. To those for whom life is like a cold, lifeless moon orbiting its way through darkness, sterile and unproductive, we who are Spirit-filled must reflect the glory of God. We are his emissaries of light and life, the means by which his unlimited love gets spread around in an unloving world.

The Spirit-filled life is contrasted in the Bible to other fillings. "Be not drunk with wine," Paul wrote, "but be filled with the Spirit" (Eph. 5:18, KJV). The quality that sets a Christian apart from the crowd is this filling. Faith for some is only skin deep, a convenient cloak of respectability. The "Christ-life" is Christian all the way through. Man looks on the outward appearance; God looks on the heart.

The Spirit-filled life is easily distinguishable: it expresses itself in music. The rich and deep expressions of hymns and spiritual songs should betray the Spirit-filled life, according to Paul (Eph. 5:19). It is no accident that the longest book of the Bible—Psalms—consists of songs. Music has aptly been called the language of the soul; it springs from the deep well waters of the Spirit-filled life.

The Spirit-filled life is also the thankful life. But the erosion of vital faith has caused society to slip as far as civil manners are concerned. Why give thanks if we are the creators of life? We have come to believe a lie if we think for one moment that life is self-made. It is not. God is the source of our being, the providential Provider of all things—including life itself. "The Spirit of God has made me," Job declared, "the breath of the Almighty gives me life" (33:4). Therefore, we give thanks.

The Spirit-filled life is also one lived in harmony with others. The Bible characterizes proper human relations as living in submission to one another. How contrary to our way of thinking. We would rather be "one up" on each other. "Submitting yourselves one to another in the fear of God" (Eph. 5:21, KJV) is the mark of the Spirit-filled life.

The Spirit-filled life must be something we deeply desire. The psalmist prayed, "Create in me a clean heart, O God, and put a new and right spirit within me" (51:10, RSV). We are the doorkeeper. God waits outside like a patient guest for the host to invite him in. "Behold, I stand at the door, and knock: if any man hear my voice, and open the door, I will come in to him, and will sup with him, and he with me" (Rev. 3:20, KJV).

G. K. Chesterton once remarked that "Christianity has not been tried and found wanting. It has been found difficult and not tried." Christ's ways are contrary to popular notions of living. Yet his ways offer a joyful release, a tantalizing possibility of a new beginning.

12
The Gentle Life

Franklin Delano Roosevelt once remarked that the reason he liked his wartime aid Harry Hopkins was because "he made so few demands." Few of us possess that trait. At one time or another we make unreasonable demands on others. It is a common human problem.

All of us admire people who could best be described as "gentle." What would our world be like if it were inhabited only by the pushy, take-charge intimidators of society? There is a biblical ideal which, if lived to the full, would make the world a better place: "Let your gentleness be evident to all" (Phil. 4:5).

A gentle person isn't one who necessarily gets shoved around all the time. Gentleness, rightly understood is a form of toughness. It is like a velvet-covered brick. A gentle person has learned to live life in moderation, not to carry things to excess. The biblical word for gentleness means, "that which is fitting, right, equitable." It is a quality Jesus possessed. No one would charge Jesus with being weak.

A gentle person is the opposite of a violent person. "All who draw the sword," Jesus said, "will die by the sword" (Matt. 26:52). Violence breeds violence and gentleness breeds gentleness. "A gentle answer," the proverb reads, "turns away wrath" (15:1). Gentleness is a fruit of the spirit, while violence is a work of the flesh.

This little gem of a word, *gentle*, occurs only seven times in the New Testament. Variously translated "forbearance," "moderation," "kindness," "reasonable," and "lenient," it acts like salve on a stinging wound. It may be difficult to translate, but it is not difficult to see the need for it.

Gentleness and meekness are traits Jesus displayed. We know this from the gospel stories and also from a reference in the Epistles. Paul pled with Corinthian Christians to show moral courage. He based his argument on how Jesus lived. "By the meekness and gentleness of Christ," Paul wrote, "I appeal to you" (2 Cor. 10:1).

Through a mosaic of Bible texts, the word paints an eloquent and powerful picture. It was sued as the basis of Paul's appeal before Felix (Acts 24:4), as a requirement for bishops (1 Tim. 3:3), as a quality for every Christian (Titus 3:2), and as the essence of divine wisdom (James 3:17). First-century slaves were instructed to submit to harsh masters as well as gentle slaveowners. Gentleness formed the seed bed for a quiet revolution that, in the end, unseated Roman tyranny.

Gentleness graces human relations like a genial guest in an ill-mannered crowd. It does not force itself on others, asks no favors, makes no demands. The gentle life is like a soft, warm breeze warming the heart and lifting the spirit. Those who display its properties often turn the tide of opinion in tough debate. The gentle, along with the meek, are the true inheritors of the earth.

A gentle person does not burn out. Gentleness is fuel for the long haul. Like a comfortable garment, gentleness cloaks the ruggedness of personal rights. It knows when to assert itself and when to use restraint.

In moments of defeat and humiliation, a gentle person nearby is better than any doctor. Gentleness nurses the wounds of crushed and broken people. It is a well-seasoned traveler on the road of life, a companion to godliness. Like a pungent herb, a little of it goes a long way. Among all the virtues we are to exhibit in light of the soon return of Christ, gentleness stands out. "Let your gentleness be evident to all. The Lord is near" (Phil. 4:5).

Above the push and shove of life, Christ invites us to stand firm, calm, and in control. Gentleness will steady our world.

13

The Common Life

The Christian life is a common life. By that we do not mean that it is plain and uninteresting. Rather, the common life is a life of brotherhood shared first with all of God's creation but uniquely with other Christians.

There is a common brotherhood among all of creation. Paul underscored this point in his powerful Mars' Hill address: "From one man he made every nation of men, that they should inhabit the whole earth.... For in him we live and move and have our being" (Acts 17:26, 28). We are his offspring. We have something in common with every living human being.

Beyond this universal brotherhood, however, there is a unique bond that Christians share. The terms *brother* and *sister* were the most popular descriptions of disciples during the first three centuries of Christian expansion. Jesus fondly used the word *brother* to describe the disciples (Matt. 23:8), and Paul called Christ "the firstborn among many brothers" (Rom. 8:29). Early Christians captured a communal spirit and rocked the world. (Actually, as G.K. Chesterton described the incredible interruption of the incarnation, it did not shake the world; it steadied it.)

Our world is terribly fragmented. The poet Yeats graphically described it as "out of joint."

> Things fall apart: the center cannot hold;
> Mere anarchy is loosed upon the world,
> The blood-rimmed tide is loosed, and everywhere
> The ceremony of innocence is drowned;
> The best lack conviction, while the worst
> Are full of passionate intensity.

Jesus calls us to live a life of unity with other Christians. On the *Via Gloriosa*, he prayed "that they all may be one...as You, Father, are in Me and I in You, that they also may be one in Us, so that the world may believe...that You have sent Me" (John 17:21, AV). Our oneness is the key to healing the fractures of our fragmented world.

The common life is not a closed life. "It is not simply to be taken for granted that the Christian has the privilege of living with other Christians," wrote theologian Dietrich Bonhoeffer. "Jesus Christ lived in the midst of his enemies." The purpose of the incarnation was to bring peace to the enemies of God. True community emerges in a context of the reconciling love of God. It touches our world.

The cloistered life isolates us from others and renders us ineffective. Martin Luther once wrote that "the kingdom is to be in the midst of your enemies." Those who would sit among roses and lilies with only the devout people do not fulfill the commission of Christ.

Christian brotherhood is not a concocted scheme to hold the troops together. Rather, it is a divine reality with Christ as its head. Thus, the common life is life lived under one Master: "The God who made the world and everything in it is the Lord of heaven and earth" (Acts 17:24). "There is one Lord," Paul instructed early disciples, "one God and Father of all" (Eph. 4:6). No sentimental collection of idealists, the church of Jesus Christ is organically linked to divine authority.

The common life is life lived with a common faith and a common salvation. This is no "write your own script" kind of thing. Its core and center is revealed truth—the Word of God. Christianity without the Bible at its center is like a tree whose ancient trunk is hollowed by decay.

The common life is a shared life. One does not lose one's identity in Christ. Quite the opposite: each gift and talent is valued just as individual parts of a human body are valued. "Do good to all," Paul told Galatian Christians (Gal. 6:10, RSV). The common life is anything but a life turned inward; the gospel is for the whole of society.

In the fifteenth century, groups emerged in Germany and the Netherlands calling themselves the Brethren of the Common Life. Their promotion of piety and godliness steadied Northern Europe during that century. Few, if any, rivaled its chief spokesman, Thomas à Kempis, in offering the language of simple, pure devotion to Jesus. "Never be idle," he wrote, "but either be reading, or writing, or praying, or meditating, or endeavoring something for the public good."

14
The Practical Life

The Christian life is an intensely practical life. Truth is given not merely to be contemplated, but to be done. "All good maxims have been written," observed Pascal. "It only remains to put them into practice." Pascal's is a powerful statement—one that inspires practical living.

Sam Jones, the colorful nineteenth-century Methodist preacher known for his commonness and total lack of pretentiousness, once remarked that "the secret of a happy life is to do your duty and trust in God." Practical Christianity cannot be more simply put than that.

Those who take the Christian life seriously do not make a great noise about it. "Make it your ambition to lead a quiet life, to mind your own business and to work with your hands," wrote the apostle Paul in First Thessalonians (4:11). It is in honest, decent work that the practical Christian experience is best fleshed out before our world.

"Man goes forth to his work and to his labor until the evening," wrote the psalmist (104:23, RSV). Six days we are to work, God said, and on the seventh we are to rest. Work and rest—both find harmony and rhythm and a noble purpose. It is through labor that faith is made visible, worlds are made better, and personal worth is fulfilled.

But what if failure comes? Does God divorce himself from failure, or is he the author of success only? Few people are aware that J. C. Penney suffered failure and defeat before forming his vast retail empire built on the golden rule. "At one time during my business career," he wrote, "I broke down both nervously and physically, and went to a sanitarium."

It sometimes takes cold, black disaster to inspire one to achieve the heights of success. A paratrooper in the Second World War lost his hands in an explosion, but went on to play the lead role in "The Best Years of Our Lives." His deep inner faith in God saw him through tough times.

Near the end of the Vietnam War a young marine came to faith in Jesus Christ. He had been a scoffer and agnostic all his life, but a tragic accident ended his unbelief. After being wounded by a concussion grenade, he listened to the Scripture being read by the chaplain whose life he had saved by taking the force of the explosion himself—and believed. After years of rejecting the gospel, his decision was, "If I'm going to be a Christian, I'm going to be one all the way!"

Practical Christian living, then, is no product of fancy talk or even obedience to a set of rules. It means living for Jesus every day, doing what we are now doing (only better), and helping others before we help ourselves. We all know far more of religion than we can ever put into practice. It is time to fulfill James's ideal: "Be doers of the word, and not hearers only" (James 1:22, RSV).

49

15
The Selfless Life

Denial of self is a central part of Christ's call to discipleship (Luke 9:23). It is also completely foreign to current thinking in our world. We are, as Evelyn Underhill has written, "drifting toward a religion which keeps its eyes on humanity rather than deity." We are in danger of elevating self over Savior. Such a stance runs contrary to the Christian faith. Jesus said, "No one can serve two masters" (Matt. 6:24, RSV). Following Christ means we must make a choice between living for ourselves or living for God.

Thomas à Kempis once wrote, "Keep this short and perfect word: Let go all and you shall find all; leave desire and you shall find rest. Weigh this thoroughly in your mind, and when you have fulfilled it you shall understand all things . . . In this short word is included the perfection of religious persons."

Renunciation of the self is contrary to our human nature. While self-preservation is instinctive, and thus legitimate, self-aggrandizement is sin. Self-esteem is normal and healthy but self-love is detrimental to the spiritual life.

God calls us to put all things in perspective. The first commandment, "Thou shalt have no other gods before me" (Exod. 20:3, KJV), forbids us from putting self above God.

"Man does not know in what rank to place himself," wrote Pascal. "He has plainly gone astray and fallen from his true place without being able to find it again." The prophet Isaiah declared, "All we like sheep have gone astray; we have turned every one to his own way" (Isa. 53:6, KJV).

Christians are called to be cultural nonconformists. Those who are captured by pleasure, who equate money with worth and sex with love miss the center of Christian teaching. God has given us all things to enjoy (1 Tim. 6:17), but always in the perspective of his lordship. The self, likewise, must come under God's gracious and liberating governance.

The one who knows God but does not know himself in relationship to God becomes proud. On the other hand, the one who despairs of himself and knows not God ends in hopelessness. Knowing God's gracious provision of mercy lifts the human spirit. The arrogant may still go their way, but the end is destruction. When the self is viewed in relationship to the loving rule of God, only then can true freedom be experienced.

Freedom to love and to help others comes only when the self is put in its proper place. In answer to the question, "Which is the greatest commandment in the law?" Jesus replied: "'Love the Lord your God with all your heart and with all your soul and with all your mind.' This is the first and greatest commandment." He did not stop there, however, but continued, "And the second is like it: 'Love your neighbor as yourself.' All the Law and the

Prophets hang on these two commandments" (Matt. 22:35–40).

Jesus taught that "whoever finds his life will lose it, and whoever loses his life for my sake will find it" (Matt. 10:39). These words inspired Jim Elliot to write in his journal, "He is no fool who gives up that which he cannot keep to gain that which he cannot lose."

What a paradox the truth becomes! Self-denial leads to fulfillment and true happiness. Peter knew this truth. At the end of his life, he wrote, "Humble yourselves...under the mighty hand of God, that he may exalt you in due time" (1 Peter 5:6, KJV). Jesus said, "Many who are first will be last, and many who are last will be first" (Matt. 19:30, NIV).

Knowing what to put first is the key to the spiritual experience. Pascal once wrote, "The last thing one knows is what to put first." Jesus came to reconcile all things unto himself, to put life in its proper order. The incarnation shows mankind the greatness of its misery and the greatness of the divine remedy. "Jesus Christ," wrote Pascal, "is therefore a God whom we approach without pride, and before whom we humble ourselves without despair."

16
The Humble Life

Humility has been called the foundation of all virtues. Easily recognized yet difficult to achieve, humility is a rare human trait but one to which a great inheritance is due. The true inheritors of the earth are the quiet, humble people of society (Matt. 5:5).

"Do not think that you have made any progress," wrote Thomas à Kempis, "unless you esteem yourself inferior to all." Such a statement at first seems shocking. Granted, there are some people whose self-esteem is so low that they are incapable of living normal, healthy lives. But genuine humility does not call for self-oblivion. Quite the contrary. It elevates our humanity to a level displayed elegantly by Jesus in his incarnation.

Jesus calls us to an honest appraisal of ourselves. "That which is highly esteemed among men," Jesus said, "is detestable in the sight of God" (Luke 16:15, NASB). "Let each esteem others better than themselves," pleaded Paul (Phil. 2:3, KJV).

The Bible tells us not to think of ourselves more highly than we ought to think. Love is to rule every relationship.

Christ's call to humility is counter to the mood of today. Our world rewards pushy, aggressive, self-assertive people. There seems to be no room for humility anymore, at least the kind that a seventeenth-century bishop described. François de La Mothe Fénelon wrote: "In order that humility be true, we need to give continual homage to God in our lowliness, and to stay in our place is to love being nothing."

The point is that our "nothing" becomes everything in Christ. All true humility grows in the rich, fertile soil of Christ's example. In his incarnation, God became man. Jesus made himself of no reputation. The cross sets the pattern for all selfless living. Jesus "humbled himself," Paul wrote, "and became obedient to death—even the death of the cross" (Phil. 2:8).

Pride always goes before a fall. It was this way from the beginning. Lucifer coveted the character of the Most High. God said he would be "brought down to the grave, to the depths of the pit" (Isa. 14:15).

God resists the proud but gives grace to the humble. "Do not be proud," said Paul, "but be willing to associate with people of low position. Do not be conceited" (Rom. 12:16).

The Bible does not teach self-annihilation. God sees us as the object of his love. Such high value helps us bring life into better perspective. "Humble yourselves," James advised, "and he will lift you up" (James 4:10). Restored to the image of God through redemption, we share the exaltation that Christ experienced in his resurrection.

Nikolaus Ludwig von Zinzendorf, whose godly example of faith and piety sparked a massive missionary movement in the eighteenth century, shared the secret of humility: "I have a great need for Christ; I have a great Christ for my need." We, like him, must accept the humbling fact that our human condition caused the incarnation. Our sin prompted salvation. To admit one needs a Savior is a humbling matter, but that is what it means to be a Christian.

The value of human life does not lie in "personal rights" but in the spiritual bond that binds and subordinates us to God and to others. Do not think that our Creator will abandon us. We can lift our heads high, not in selfish pride, but in confidence that God has rescued us from sin and our own egos.

The humble life reshapes our world. It does not cause us to withdraw into a shriveled, inward melancholy. Rather, it leaps with the joy of liberation. To be humble is to regain a true perspective on life.

Pride says, "I must be first." Humility says, "God and others are not to take the back seat." The mystery of it all is that true fulfillment and happiness come when God and others are given preference and due honor.

The humble life takes the gospel seriously. It recognizes Christ's demand for honesty, purity, love, and selflessness.

17
The Silent Life

There is a time to be silent—so goes the proverb. Few of us ever carve out the time to be silent, however. Silence poses a greater threat than we can hope to bear. Give us noise, we say, to cover the poverty of an empty mind and an even emptier soul.

We have become so accustomed to noise that its absence is deafening. Conflict, loneliness, and despondency are masked by the diversion of noise. This is why the love of solitude is incomprehensible. To be silent is to deal with our inner thoughts and that is too painful for most.

Many have applauded the healing quality of silence. Thomas à Kempis discovered that "in silence and in stillness a devout soul profits and learns the hidden things of the Scriptures." Thomas Merton ventured that in our era of violence and unrest we should rediscover meditation, inner prayer, and "creative Christian silence." Even the Swiss psychiatrist Paul Tournier lauded silence as a mark of true dependence on God. Others have found it to be the only safe retreat from the spiritually numbing effects of noise.

The Bible reveals how silence is truly "golden." It allows us to listen to God. Elijah discovered this in a silent cave. Plagued by fear and loneliness he heard the still, small voice of God (1 Kings 19:12). "Be still," God whispers, "and know that I am God" (Ps. 46:10).

Those who fail to carve out creative moments of silence are prime candidates for restlessness. Peace follows those who shut the door and call on Jesus. "If I were a doctor and were asked for advice," said the famous Danish philosopher Sören Kierkegaard, "I should reply: create silence! Bring men to silence. The word cannot be heard in the world of today."

Silence sets the stage for serious encounter with God. "Come apart and rest awhile," Jesus invites. Faith demands quiet confidence. In times of silence our faith is strengthened. Silence helps us concentrate on a purpose that fulfills our deeper needs as well as reveals God's intention for us.

Silence helps us disconnect with the familiar. It is precisely this disconnection that we need because the familiar often deadens and dulls spiritual sensitivity. We are daily bombarded with so many messages, advertisements, voices calling for our money, attention, or loyalty. Our only effective method of coping with the proliferation of words is selective inattention. We "tune out" the noise and in the process stand the risk of missing a life-changing message.

Silence helps us recover perspective. Perspective allows us to sift the urgent from the unnecessary, the important from the trivial. It helps us draw together dissipated energies and a fragmented existence.

One can be silent in a crowd but it is easier to be

silent when we are alone. Distraction is the enemy of spiritual concentration. "He therefore who intends to attain to the more inward and spiritual things of religion," wrote à Kempis, "must with Jesus depart from the multitude."

What are the disciplines of silence and how may these be achieved? First, carve out time alone with your Creator. God invites it. Remember that before the Fall God walked in the garden with the first man and woman in the cool of the evening. "Real silence, real stillness, really holding one's tongue," wrote Bonhoeffer, "comes only as the sobering consequence of spiritual stillness."

Set realistic goals. Silence for a day may be an impossibility. Try it for an hour. Keep a journal of your thoughts and insights.

Seek out a special quiet place. Korean Christians have a long tradition of retreating to the mountains for prayer, fasting, and meditation. Your own personal "mountain" may be a corner of a garden, a special room alone.

Set no agenda other than to listen to God. Remember, however, that he speaks through prayer and the Word. Silence is not a vacuum to be filled with vague, mystical nothingness. It is like a quiet brook whose waters tumble over the rocks of our stoney hearts, cleansing and refreshing us.

There are places in the memory of my heart where God and I have often met. They span the world—a stream in Korea, a narrow rocky ledge in Yosemite, a bluff in the Blue Ridge Mountains, a beach in the Philippines, seats on planes, my own garden and study. You too can find God and yourself through silence.

18
The Temporal Life

Time is the boundary of everything we experience. Things seen are temporal; things unseen are eternal. Through the centuries this kind of wisdom has sifted down to us mortals. The eternal God concerns himself with time as well as eternity.

Time is the most valuable possession we have. In the end, it is not money in banks, security in possessions, or even high standing in life, but *time* that is valued most.

When the artist Picasso celebrated his ninetieth birthday he was asked what he would like most in life. His answer: "Give me more time."

The Bible is not silent on the subject. Time is the very creation of God himself. He who is called the Ancient of Days created all things, visible or invisible (Col. 1:16). Solomon in sagelike fashion viewed this rare and vanishing commodity and declared, "There is a time for everything, and a season for every activity under heaven" (Eccles. 3:1).

There is no emptiness to time. God fills it with his presence whether or not we recognize it. Ever since the incarnation of Jesus Christ, time has taken on new meaning. The God who began it all invaded our time and space. Have you ever stopped

59

to think that in his humanity Jesus voluntarily limited himself to temporal territory?

The careless, reckless way that most people spend time is shocking. Horace Mann, the father of American education, once placed a classified ad in a New York paper: "Lost, yesterday, somewhere between sunrise and sunset, two golden hours, each set with diamond minutes. No reward offered, for they are gone forever."

In each bank account of one day there is deposited 86,400 seconds. Each night, whatever is left of this time is canceled out. Those wasted seconds are gone forever. The Bible tells us to make "the most of every opportunity, because the days are evil" (Eph. 5:16).

There is no way to transfer unused time to tomorrow or to a bank account. Therefore, we are warned by the proverb not to boast of tomorrow, "for you do not know what a day may bring forth" (Prov. 27:1).

James asked the question, "What is your life?" His reply is disturbing in its candor. "You are a mist that appears for a little while and then vanishes," he wrote (James 4:14).

The psalmist David prayed to God, "O Lord, what is man that you care for him?" He answered his own question with blunt realism: "Man is like a breath; his days are like a fleeting shadow" (Ps. 144:3, 4).

While time must be viewed as an extremely valued commodity, eternity is to be treasured even more. "Set your minds on things above," Paul warned, "not on earthly things" (Col. 3:2).

The temporal life has meaning only in light of

the purpose toward which all time and history move. "So we fix our eyes not on what is seen," the Bible teaches, "but on what is unseen. For what is seen is temporary, but what is unseen is eternal" (2 Cor. 4:18).

We need to view time from this perspective. Life lived now should reflect God's timeless values. The greatest of these values is love. It never goes out of style. It will never cease. Only when our lives are lived under Christ's loving leadership can we ever hope to experience and give true love.

19
The Resurrected Life

The English writer and poet T. S. Eliot once asked, "Where is the life we have lost in living?" We are always getting ready to live but rarely live life to the full.

Most of us take life in stride. Years pile on years and life has a habit of slipping by. The young rarely think of mortality, and the assured barely give it a passing thought. "Who is the man who desires life, and loves many days?" asked the psalmist. "Depart from evil, and do good; seek peace, and pursue it" (Ps. 34:12, 14, NKJB).

There is one event that changed the course of history and which holds the key to purposeful living. That event is the resurrection of Jesus Christ from the dead, a miracle that made it possible for us to recover life in our living.

Critics of the gospel account try to argue the resurrection into oblivion. Yet it rises as the peak event of the Christian faith. Jesus himself predicted it, the empty tomb attests to it, and our world is the better for it.

Life's purpose is inextricably bound up in the resurrection of Christ from the dead. Without this triumph over tragedy we are to be pitied (1 Cor.

15:19) and our faith is futile. The first disciples were fired with zeal by this fact of history, and our hope in life after death depends on it.

The Easter story is simply that Jesus lives and so shall we. No concoction of fanciful imagination, the resurrection is sober history. Through it Jesus has been declared to be both Lord and Christ (Acts 2:36). By it he overcame death and evil. As first-born from the dead he was acclaimed head of all things, including his church. The resurrection is the capstone of our salvation and is the advance notice that we too will rise again at the final resurrection.

Ultimate meaning and destiny are tied up in Jesus. "I am come that (you) might have life," Jesus said (John 10:10, KJV).

Life is either a random collection of unrelated incidents or one with a design and purpose. Those who opt for the first explanation must find meaning for the moment. Those who choose the latter discover faith for the long haul.

At the tag ending of the 1960s, a young graduate of Mills College addressed her graduating class. The title of her speech made national news: "The Future Is a Hoax." Combine this with the dictum of industrialist Henry Ford, "History is bunk," and you have a description of an empty life. When left with a purposeless history and an even bleaker future, what philosophy of life is left?

> "Let us eat and drink
> for tomorrow we die." (1 Cor. 15:32)

Faith unlocks the door to answers to life's ultimate questions. It rolls back the stone of unbelief

63

and boldly declares, "Jesus lives, and so shall we." Neither futility nor indulgence fit a life of faith.

Our calling, in part at least, is to reverse the pessimism of our day. There is hope in Christ. The resurrected life of Jesus, which we share by faith, is one filled with bright optimism and expectancy. "Just as Christ was raised from the dead," Paul wrote, "we too may live a new life" (Rom. 6:4).

Ralph Waldo Emerson once wrote, "Great men are they who see that spiritual is stronger than any material force, that thoughts rule the world." The resurrected life is one of those ideas. It captivates, rules, and then liberates us.

After a long and explosive life of creative activity, Leonardo da Vinci remarked, "While I thought I was learning how to live, I have been learning how to die." He learned what everyone must learn, that death is certain. This is no surprise to a Christian.

Learning both to live and to die is our agenda for life. If we fail to grasp the significance of the resurrection we risk losing our grip on these two realities. The event is fixed in history; the dynamic is potent for eternity.

20

The Unselfish Life

Christianity is in danger of selling its soul to the prevailing culture. In the name of relevance it has adopted the norms of society. Prophets of relevance call Christians to bend with the times, to blend with the moods and popular notions of the day.

In sixteenth-century German Saxony, a monk named Martin Luther wrote a trilogy of books exposing the evils of religious exploitation by a corrupted hierarchy. One of these he titled the *Babylonian Captivity of the Church*. His point was clear. True faith had been taken prisoner by fakes and phonies. We are in danger of the same thing today, only the attack does not come from a corrupted church but from our American culture.

Nowhere is this more evident than in pop psychology which extols self-affirmation over self-denial. The debate is stacked and quite unfair. Those who have sold their soul to the company store, so to speak, charge that Christ's call for self-denial denigrates authentic personhood. Why, they ask, should we let other people set the agenda for our lives?

Granted there are some people who are weak and who do not possess the ability to be self-assertive when they need to be. Lacking a healthy self-image they let others exploit them. But whatever happened to the biblical virtues of turning the other cheek, going the extra mile, giving the cloak also, and offering a cup of cold water?

Somehow the prevailing culture offers a plastic substitute for the real prize. What is it that Paul pressed toward and hoped to attain? I doubt if it was more perks, benefits, or even a protected ego. I even seriously doubt if it was the freedom to find himself, to do his own thing. He had learned his lesson from Jesus: "He who finds his life will lose it, and he who loses his life for my sake will find it" (Matt. 10:39, RSV).

Christians are called to be counter culture. Our kingdom is always of another world. This does not mean that we deny our cultural roots and adopt monastic asceticism. (Paul deals with such a stance in Colossians 2:20 ff.) To be counter culture is to attack sinfulness on all fronts. That which invades social institutions and the human heart, which denies justice, dehumanizes persons, and destroys love must be overcome.

Christ's invitation to discipleship is terribly attractive when stacked up against the slavery of self-adulation. Jesus told us that his yoke is easy and his burden is light. True discipleship is not marked by extremes of devotion and self-abasement. These, Paul declares, have no value in checking the indulgence of the flesh (Col. 2:23, RSV).

Life in Christ means that our real identity is now established and our true self protected. Changed into the image of Christ, we are freed to become servants to all.

What would it be like to call the crowd of witnesses

mentioned in Hebrews 12:1 to give testimony to the selfless life? And could those who promote and sanction self-liberation stomach the sheer joy of martyrs, heroes of the faith, and just plain Christians?

"To this you have been called," Peter writes, "because Christ also suffered for you, leaving you an example, that you should follow in His steps" (1 Pet. 2:21, RSV). The words which follow in those next verses paint a scene so counter to what the self-affirmation movement calls virtuous as to be shocking in contrast. "I have yet to meet someone who has truly lived a selfless life who has not experienced great joy and fulfillment," wrote a missionary doctor from Africa.

Isn't it time to expose the fallacy of our own Babylonian captors? All the catchphrases of narcissism—"watch out for number one," "do your own thing," "let it all hang out"—need to be buried with a fitting epigraph placed on the tombstone:

> Here lies a counterfeit whose motto was "self above service;" for the real model, look to Jesus—service above self!

21
The Ordinary Life

Life has a way of being terribly ordinary. Those who look for sounding brass and crashing cymbals are in for disappointment. Life is full of dull routines.

For the most part, the things that Jesus did were ordinary also. Sometimes we think that all he ever did was perform miracles, yet some of his greatest accomplishments were not dramatic events, but rather changed attitudes, shifted values, transformed behavior.

Take, for instance, his washing of the disciples' feet in the upper room only hours before his betrayal by Judas and execution on a Roman cross. What Jesus did was something common in that day, yet his action contained a radical twist—reversing the social order of master and servant. "Lord," Peter responded with enlightened understanding, "not my feet only but also my hands and my head" (John 13:9, RSV).

"Give me a drink," Jesus said to a woman at a well in Samaria. What a common setting for one of life's great lessons! Startled by the reversal of custom, the woman listened intently to Jesus' discourse on eternal life. Her reply reflected a miracle within: "Sir, give me this water, that I may not thirst" (John 4:15, RSV).

Years ago Robert Murray McCheyne remarked about how we turn again for advice to those who have mastered the spiritual secrets of life. Such is true today; distant voices of the past speak with remarkable clarity.

One of those voices is that of Brother Lawrence, a seventeenth-century Christian who mastered the doctrine of the ordinary. He wrote, "The time of business does not with me differ from the time of prayer; and in the noise and clutter of my kitchen, while persons are at the same time calling for different things, I possess God in as great tranquility as if I were upon my knees."

The soul that wants to know God can practice the presence of God. But the secret is wanting to know God. Life, we think, would become easier if God were to break in on our conscious awareness with loud messages, bright lights, and brilliant movements. But God does not usually stage his presence. True, he did so in cloud and fire in the wilderness for ancient Hebrews, but for most of us he chooses to reveal himself in the ordinary things of life— duty, habit, the menial and the mundane.

Yet when God is present, nothing remains usual, common, or ordinary. "The things Jesus did," said Oswald Chambers in his lectures to YMCA students early in this century, "were of the most menial and commonplace order, and this is an indication that it takes all God's power in me to do the most commonplace things his way."

That is it! Doing common things Jesus' way. How remarkably exciting life can become when this truth

69

is lived. The usual becomes the unusual, the routine becomes special, and the natural is transformed into the supernatural.

"Do not always scrupulously confine yourself to certain rules, or particular forms of devotion," concluded Brother Lawrence, "but act with a general confidence in God, with love and humility."

"And whatever you do or say, let it be as a representative of the Lord Jesus, and come with him into the presence of God the Father to give him your thanks." (Col. 3:17, LB)

22
The Contemplative Life

The Christian life is a reflective experience. Thinking is part of the game plan. Plato once observed that "the life which is unexamined is not worth living." Long before Greek philosophers captured the mind of the ancient world, the psalmist gave good advice: "Stand in awe, and sin not: commune with your own heart upon your bed, and be still" (Ps. 4:4, KJV). Later Paul was to write, "Examine yourselves to see whether you are in the faith." (2 Cor. 13:5).

Thoughts are like windows of the soul. As a man thinks, so is he, the proverb reads (Prov. 23:7). Daniel Webster believed that the mind is a great lever of things and that human thought is the process by which human ends are answered. Christians are called to bring every thought into captivity to Christ (2 Cor. 10:5).

The peril of our times is that there is tragically little time to think. We fill our lives full of activity without building upon the firm foundation of serious reflection. The contemplative acreage is missing in most of us. Even when present it is often squandered in idle thoughts. Francois Mauride once wrote: "The nobility of every thinking person lies in the power of mastering himself through reflection."

The path to serious reflection calls for a commitment to meditation. Such activity is not random, drifting, or unfocused. Christian meditation fixes the soul on God. Imagine one solitary hour alone without a radio, music, background noise, or any distraction. What would your thoughts be like? Would they be random, undisciplined, and scattered? Or would they be focused, directed toward God, reflective, and purposeful?

The meditative dimensions of life defy neat rules. The only rule is one of response. Life is like wind in trees: storms and stress bend the trunks and snap the branches; Christians are called to reflect on these stresses, to grow sturdy through them, and to stand tall in adversity. Thinking and reflecting on life from a perspective of faith matures us. How we respond to life's events indicates the depths of our devotion to God. Charles Swindoll writes, "If thinking God's way in the suddenness of storms makes our faith grow broad, then trusting God's wisdom in the dailyness of living makes it grow deep."

Meditation works best in solitude. The cultivation of silence and solitude provides the arena for focused thinking. Carving out little retreats in life allows time for reflection. Aloneness does not always guarantee solitude; one can even find it in crowds. The ability to shut out the din of life and to gain a godly perspective on things helps us grow.

Solitude needs no defense. It only needs to be understood. Solitude is really an attitude as much as it is seclusion from society. It is the objective fact of detachment. Admittedly, withdrawal from the pressures of life for a time helps us gain new handles on living. But not everyone can go to mountains, caves, or deserts to pray and to think. Christ calls us to reality, not retreat.

There must be depth to our contemplation. Surface thinking robs the soul of any true meaning. Historic Christianity rests on truth—not truth as an abstract concept or a mystical encounter. Thus, true meditation finds its framework in the Scriptures. One of this century's greatest theologians, J. Gresham Machen, wrote a book titled *What is Faith?* His words are still appropriate fifty years after he wrote them: "A marked characteristic of the present day is a lamentable intellectual decline, which has appeared in all fields of human endeavor except those that deal with purely material things." Only through the primacy of truth will the contemplative life find its true focus.

The Christian is called to think thoughts shaped by the Bible. Thoughts, if they are to be useful to advance the kingdom, must never remain shut up inside ourselves. The windows of the soul are to be opened outward. In reality, the contemplative life then becomes the practical life, touching a world with the tender compassion of Christ and the fire of conviction.

23
The Eternal Life

Why is it that only the elderly and terminally ill seem to appreciate eternity? Could it be that suffering and the certainty of death distill a wisdom known by few who are young and self-assured? A ninety-one-year-old woman living out the richness of her years asked me one day, "When are you going to write on the eternal life? That is the real life, you know." Her question drove me to probe this timely subject.

Eternity seems so far off, so unreal, a subject for philosophers and theologians. The mere thought of the afterlife, to many, is an outright denial of life itself. Who wants to be so heavenly-minded that they are of no earthly good? Yet the notion that life never really ends with the grave haunts every living person. Each of us must come to grips with eternity. Only when that is done can we get on with living.

Not all understand a Christian view of life and eternity. When one reads Psalm 90, it appears that even Moses was gripped with the seeming futility of life. "We spend our years as a tale that is told," he wrote (Ps. 90:9, KJV). Seventy years or eighty years are given us but even the best of those years are often marked by emptiness and pain. "It is soon cut off," Moses concluded, "and we fly away" (Ps. 90:10, NASB).

Who hasn't at one time or other thought the thoughts of Shakespeare's character Macbeth?

> Life's but a shadow, a poor player,
> That struts and frets his hour upon the stage,
> And then is heard no more; it is a tale
> Told by an idiot, full of sound and fury,
> Signifying nothing.

In contrast to the empty meaning some give to that elusive quantity we call "time," the Bible presents a clear picture of eternity. In fact, reading the Bible is like taking a deep breath of eternity. Eternal life, so the Bible teaches, is something to be laid hold of, hoped for, and experienced now. The righteous will go into it, and the unredeemed will not. It is synonymous with knowing God and is the direct result of faith in Jesus Christ. It may not be purchased, worked for, or gained by any amount of religious duty. In practical terms, the eternal life encompasses all that God intends for us both now and in the eternal state.

Eternal life is the inheritance of all who believe in Jesus. It is a gift from God. Those who love their life will lose it, Jesus said, and those who hate it in this world will keep it unto life eternal (John 12:25). "One thing you lack," Jesus told the rich ruler who sought eternal life. "Go and sell all you possess...and you shall have treasure in heaven; and come, follow Me" (Mark 10:21, NASB). Eternal life is difficult to grasp for those who try to hang onto this world and its possessions.

From the moment of conversion to Christ, God imparts the full and rich vitality of eternal life. It is more than life after death. It is a present reality as well (cf. 1 John 5:11–13).

Life takes on value only when it is nothing less than the life of God. "This is eternal life," Jesus said, "that they may know you, the only true God" (John 17:3). Possessing eternal life is really sharing the character of God himself.

The most important thing to know about eternal life is that God is its author. Time is what he created in the beginning. Eternity is what God is in his character. "From everlasting to everlasting thou art God," wrote Moses (Ps. 90:2, rsv). It is beyond human reason to understand fully how God shares this quality with his creation, yet he does that freely through his eternal Son.

As author and finisher of our faith, Jesus Christ is the architect of eternal life. Centuries ago, Thomas à Kempis, writing in his tiny library in Zwolle, stated the essence of eternal life as focused in Jesus. What better commentary is there than his thoughts on John 14:6: "I am the way, the truth, and the life. Without the way, there is no going; without the truth, there is no knowing; without the life, there is no living."

Time tarnishes everything, but love, hope, and peace abide. These are the essence of the eternal life. It is the gift of love that orients the soul to God and it is hope that puts spring into our souls. Peace becomes the ultimate inheritance of those who know the Prince of Peace.

24
The Caring Life

The Christian life is a caring life. Compassion, a missing commodity in our time, is part and parcel of the new life in Christ. Our calling, at least in part, is to attack the inherent selfishness of our generation.

The Bible exposes the loneliness of the human condition and offers the deep fulfillment of faith in God's providential care. In his distress, David cried out, "No one cares for my soul" (Ps. 142:4 NASB). Despite Job's intense suffering, he declared, "Thy care has preserved my spirit" (Job 10:12, NASB).

The caring life is rooted in the character of God. The calm, majestic currents of authentic faith flow from their source in his love. Wisely we teach the young to recite the Bible truth, "He cares for you" (1 Peter 5:7, NASB), and confidently we sing Frank Graeff's refrain, "O yes, He cares, I know He cares!"

The caring life, however, involves risk. Jesus taught this in the story of the Good Samaritan. It is a fact of life that every human relationship involves risk. Dietrich Bonhoeffer, writing from a Nazi prison, knew that words are cheaper than actions. To a friend he wrote: "It seems to me more important actually to share someone's distress than to use smooth words about it."

No one would deny the wrenching problems of poverty, human suffering, and deprivation. Yet another kind of poverty exists; it is the poverty of the soul. Mother Teresa once told a *Time* reporter viewing her work among the poor of India, "Loneliness and the feeling of being unwanted is the most terrible poverty." It is exactly at this point that Christianity provides an answer. The love of neighbor simply means being able to ask, "What are you going through?"

Beyond the question must also come some act of caring. It was said of General William Booth, founder of the Salvation Army, that "one secret of his greatness was his sympathy and his unaffected love of mankind." Booth, as well as others who have followed the example of Jesus, effectively wedded social action with Christian witness of the gospel.

The caring life is an unselfish life. A widow I know continues a practice she and her husband began early in their marriage. Every day she gives something away to someone else. Years ago as a student I was touched by the couple's kindness, being invited often to their home. This woman's whole life has been exactly what the gospel requires— an act of giving and caring.

The caring life is one whose dependency is in the sufficiency of Christ. Oddly enough, Scripture uses the same word to express care for others as it does unhealthy anxiety. Jesus warned, "Do not be anxious about your life" (Matt. 6:25, RSV), and Paul exhorted, "Do not be anxious about anything" (Phil. 4:6). In the parable of the sower Jesus spoke of seed choked by the cares of this life (Luke 8:14), and in a plea for watchfulness, warned us not to be overtaken by the anxieties and cares of this life (Luke 21:34). Yet we are urged to care for one another (1 Cor. 12:25). Somehow the Christian must learn to bear the burden of others (Gal. 6:2) while not being burdened by the cares of living.

At the end of a fruitful life of caring, William Booth was buried with high honor. Royalty attended his funeral. Next to the queen sat a shabbily-dressed woman who placed a flower on the casket as it passed by. "How did you know him?" asked the queen. The woman's answer was simply, "He cared for the likes of us." Dare we learn the lesson of the Master? Our emotions must conform to his. What he loved we must love. How he cared, we too must care.

25
The Balanced Life

The Christian experience is often like a tire out of balance. It is prone to lopsidedness, extremes, often lacking a clear sense of direction. "A double-minded man," wrote James, is "unstable in all his ways" (James 1:8, RSV).

The balanced life is really the life of faith. It combines what we believe with what we do and makes sure that they are the same. Faith that doesn't show itself by good works is no faith at all—it is dead and useless. The walk of faith is always to be balanced by the work of faith.

Martin Luther once drew an earthy analogy to explain the balance of faith and works. He described it as a drunk on a horse, first tipping to one side, then to another. Truth bears a resemblance to that rider as well. We can so easily emphasize one dimension of it to the exclusion of another. For that reason Paul wrote the Ephesian Christians, "I urge you to live a life worthy of the calling you have received" (Eph. 4:1).

The balanced life is the mature life in Christ. Our superficial piety must give way to genuine devotion to the Savior. Indifference must yield to zeal and what the Scriptures call steadfastness (1 Cor. 15:58).

Spiritual maturity is not achieved easily; it often comes through suffering and experiencing adversity. It is an illusion that growth in grace and knowledge of our Lord and Savior Jesus Christ (2 Peter 3:18) is without struggle.

There are two distinct dangers to avoid when contemplating the goal of a balanced life. Some Christians engage in a flight from responsibility. They think that if their vocabulary is correct then they have achieved the pinnacle of spiritual achievement. They forget that knowing or saying are not the same as practical obedience.

In Jesus' day the scribes and the Pharisees were like that. Against their smug pride of perfectionism Jesus brought his most devastating judgment: "They say things, and do not do them" (Matt. 23:3, NASB). In another place Jesus quoted Isaiah, saying, "These people honor me with their lips, but their hearts are far from me" (Matt. 15:8).

The second danger is equally devastating. It is the danger of discouragement. The goal may appear too unachievable, too idealistic and impossible. We must balance our fears with our faith. "Perfect love casts out fear," John wisely wrote (1 John 4:18, NASB).

The balanced life combines two essential ingredients—common sense and uncommon sense. God has given us both; the first by natural intelligence and the second by divine enablement. Common sense, a commodity strangely missing in many, only goes so far. It cannot gain wisdom. That is from God.

Uncommon sense is born of the Spirit. It is part of our newness in Christ. "Wisdom from above," James wrote, "is first pure, then peaceable, gentle,

81

reasonable, full of mercy and good fruits, unwavering, without hypocrisy" (James 3:17, NASB).

Spiritual equilibrium is gained only by focusing on Jesus. François Fénelon, whose love for the Lord, common sense, and deep spirituality moved seventeenth-century France, once wrote:

> Jesus, I want to follow the road you have taken.
> I want to imitate you; I can only do so by your grace.

26
The Spiritual Life

Religion is often like veneer on cheap furniture. Scratch the surface and you expose the same old unregenerate self. Vital faith, unlike surface religion, is genuine to the core. True substance and spirituality go hand in hand. Reality is the goal.

Jesus said that a tree is known by its fruit (Matt. 12:33), and Paul described a Christian by the fruit of the Spirit. In each case the inner life produces visible external virtues. This is why Christianity is often referred to as a life rather than a religion.

Life that draws deeply from springs of living water will never dry up. Jesus said, "Whoever drinks of the water I shall give him will never thirst. But the water that I give him will become in him a well of water springing up into everlasting life" (John 4:14, NKJB).

If you consider what you are within, you will not care what others say of you. Thomas à Kempis once wrote, "What you are, that you are; neither by words can you be made greater than what you are in the sight of God." People judge by appearance; God weighs the motives of the heart (1 Sam. 16:7).

The spiritual experience in its simplest form is living the Christ-life. God's Holy Spirit indwells Christians and fills their lives with the aroma of

Christ. The spiritual life involves both a rest and a quest, a victory and a battle, wholeness in Christ and a progressive maturity in faith. It is the life of the Spirit on display. It is neither the concoction of a clever mind nor a mere outward conformity to a moral code. It is what the Scripture describes as walking in the Spirit. "The difference between a religion of mere letter and form and one of life and power," wrote R.A. Torrey, "lies in knowing the Holy Spirit."

If the easel is unsteady, the painter is unable to produce a clear picture. When we are selfish, self-centered, and sinful, then the Master Painter cannot produce the clear image of himself on our lives. In *A Short and Very Easy Method of Prayer*, Madame Guyon (1648–1717) wrote, "When God becomes so fully Master and Lord in us that nothing resists His dominion, then our interior is His kingdom."

The decay of internal piety is unquestionably the source of moral defection. "The confident secularism of the fifties and sixties has passed," states Colin Williams of Yale Divinity School. "People are asking questions about what is transcendent, what is life's meaning."

A genuine return to the spiritual experience is America's only hope. But if it is to produce lasting results in our society it must be a spiritual experience produced by God's Holy Spirit.

27
The Confident Life

Confidence, for the Christian, is not a brassy cockiness. Rather, it flows from deep springs of faith in the living God. Based on the settled conviction that the destiny of the human soul is bound up in God's gracious gift of eternal life, confidence finds its focus in God rather than mankind. Solomon wisely wrote, "The Lord will be your confidence" (Prov. 3:26, RSV). Such a perspective promotes courage, stimulates joy, prompts peace, and builds hope.

There is no simple formula for the confident life, no quick fix for our anxiety-prone way of living. Faith for the moment and faith for the long haul are gifts from God.

The confident life grows out of the rich soil of life lived in the Scriptures. In the Psalm of the Two Ways (Ps. 1), the righteous person is contrasted with the ungodly. One person is likened to a tree planted by streams of water; the other person is compared to chaff blown away in the wind. "His delight is in the law of the LORD," sang the psalmist about the righteous individual, "and on his law he meditates day and night" (Ps. 1:2, RSV).

Just as man is a stubborn seeker of meaning, he is also a persistent seeker of confidence. Deep within all is the need for certainty. There is a longing for peace and a sense of self-assurance. This quest finds no ultimate satisfaction within ourselves. Christ alone can bring the confidence of sins forgiven, destiny assured, meaning fulfilled.

God calls us to confident living. "Do not throw away your confidence," wrote the writer of Hebrews (10:35, RSV). In an earlier chapter he had urged his readers to "hold firmly to the faith we profess" (Heb. 4:14). Such assurance feeds on a sound theology and a realistic view of our human condition. The whole story of mankind can be summed up in these words: specially created, deeply fallen, greatly loved.

Confidence is not a transient emotion. Rather, it is settled conviction. Life for many is like a roller coaster, moving from highs to lows on a fast track. Not so the ideal of faith. "Being confident of this," Paul wrote, "that he who began a good work in you will carry it on to completion until the day of Christ Jesus" (Phil. 1:6, RSV).

The confident life waits expectantly for the ultimate reward—the mercy of God at the second coming of Christ (2 Tim. 1:18). John Calvin urged his followers to cast all the confidence of their souls on the mercy of God. Centuries earlier, Jude gave good advice: "Keep yourselves in God's love as you wait for the mercy of our Lord Jesus Christ to bring you to eternal life" (Jude 21).

Malcolm Muggeridge, the famous British newscaster, once reflected on his confidence in Jesus Christ. He was asked by the press what he wanted most to do with the little that remained of his life. His reply: "I should like my light to shine, even if only fitfully, like a match struck in a dark, cavernous night and then flickering out."

The German philosopher Goethe once wrote, "Give me your certainties; I have enough doubts of my own." In a world full of despair and uncertainty, Christians are called to give an answer to everyone who asks the reason for the hope within them (1 Peter 3:15). Such an answer will reflect the certainty of vital faith in God: "In quietness and in confidence shall be your strength" (Isa. 30:15, kjv).

28
The Indifferent Life

The task of the church is to change the spirit of the age—not to capture it or be captured by it. Admittedly it is easier to go with the flow, to let the world squeeze you into its mold.

There is a price to pay for attempting to change things. Martyrs and reformers paid with their lives and reputations. But there is an even higher price for indifference. Robert F. Dugan, head of the Washington Office of Public Affairs for the National Association of Evangelicals, charges that "the moral crisis in our land is the high cost of indifference."

Indifference, the detached stance of doing nothing, is a curse of our times. There is no lack of recruits in the company of the uncommitted.

Jesus calls us to be salt and light in our world. "You are the salt of the earth," he taught in his great sermon on the mountain (Matt. 5:13). In tandem order he affirmed, "You are the light of the world," (5:14). In these two metaphors the Master summed up the sphere of personal and corporate Christian involvement.

People talk a lot these days about relevance. But a relevant gospel is a contradiction in terms. The gospel message in and of itself is life-transforming.

Any other message is not the gospel. Christ would not have charged us with being "salt" and "light" if the gospel were something other than good news to all hurting segments of society.

The only thing irrelevant is a warped and distorted use of the gospel. Jesus set the pace for his church and we must walk in his steps.

At the outset of his ministry Jesus announced:

"The Spirit of the Lord is on me,
   because he has anointed me
   to preach good news to the poor.
   He has sent me to proclaim freedom for the prisoners
   and recovery of sight for the blind,
to release the oppressed,
   to proclaim the year of the Lord's favor."
(Luke 4:18, 19).

Can Christians afford to be indifferent in the face of poverty and other wrenching problems in the world? Should not the announced reason for the incarnation of Christ at least set part of the Christian agenda for our age? Developing a responsible social ethic is a task for our times.

Just where does one draw the line between Christian faith and social action? The truth is that there is no line. Properly understood, the two are one.

This does not mean that we equate Christian belief with partisan politics or with one approach to achieving social justice. But it does mean that our words of faith must be backed up by specific works of faith. If we love Jesus we must love the world in tangible ways—ways that touch the poor, the

89

brokenhearted, the captives and bruised of our world.

The nineteenth-century English preacher Charles Haddon Spurgeon was once asked to reconcile the problem of Christian involvement in social action. He told his inquirers to keep one foot at the cross and to reach out with the other and draw as wide a circle as possible. The radius of our Christian responsibility is as big as the heart of God and as wide as the compassion of Christ.

The Bible sets the agenda for Christian involvement. We are to obey just laws and pay taxes (Rom. 13:1–7; 1 Peter 2:13–17). We are to pray faithfully for peace and order (1 Tim. 2:1, 2). Involved first-century Christians transformed society by refusing to be indifferent.

No passage in all the Bible sums up our Christian duty more simply than the word of the prophet Micah: "He has showed you, O man, what is good. And what does the Lord require of you? To act justly and to love mercy and to walk humbly with your God" (Mic. 6:8).

Dare we reverse the tide of indifference? We are not called to bring in the kingdom or to create a utopia on earth. Only Christ can bring the kingdom to earth in its fullness. He will do that at his second coming. But we must be about kingdom business.

Ralph Waldo Emerson was no close friend of faith. His intellect, wit, and words ranged the scope of human thought. Yet he had keen insight into the biblical mandate to be doers of the Word and not hearers only. In an essay on self-reliance he wrote, "Every stoic was a stoic; but in Christendom where is the Christian?" He recognized a common truth that few of us really live that which we profess.

Indifference will bring our world to ruin and the church to weakness. Involvement means we practice what we preach. "Go put your creed into your deed," wrote Emerson. Only then will the relevant gospel change the course and tide of history.

29

The Doubting Life

Doubt is the doorway to faith. "He who claims never to have doubted does not know what faith is," wrote Paul Tournier in *The Person Reborn*, "for faith is forged through doubt."

Honest doubts are better than calculated unbelief. The former invites answers; the latter shuts the door to truth. Take Thomas, for example. His doubt invited the Master's own special blessing on all who would believe in him. "Because you have seen me," Jesus said to Thomas, "you have believed; blessed are those who have not seen and yet have believed" (John 20:29).

Those who faith is shallow are easily uprooted by unsettling doubt. A barrage of attacks threatens to dislodge them from the foundation of faith. "Did God really say...?" taunted the serpent in the Garden of Eden (Gen. 3:1). That same pattern of questioning persists today. We are tempted, as Jesus was tempted in the wilderness, to abandon our settled convictions about God's Word.

Doubt, however, fails to evict God from heaven. His unchanging character is not manipulated by the ups and downs of our faith. On the other hand, the rigid and blind dogma of unbelief only serves to make people miserable. It is also ineffective. Denying that there is a God is like trying to swallow the sea or wiping away the horizon.

"The fool has said in his heart, 'There is no God,'" wrote the psalmist (53:1, NASB). Such a label is fitting for the outright atheist, but what of those whose questions are honest, searching, and probing?

Have you learned to share your spiritual doubts? Many Christians have been made to feel that to express a doubt is to step over the line into unbelief. Such is far from the case. Doubt is not accusation. It becomes that only by a conscious act of the will. There is a difference between concluding that there is no God and questioning whether or not there is a God.

Thomas Carlyle once wrote of those who grope painfully in darkness or uncertain light and who pray vehemently for the dawn to ripen into day. His advice was that one should not doubt God, but rather, act on the beliefs one *has*, trusting God to unveil his truth.

The Christian experience is not one of perfect knowledge. If this were true we would be like God, possessing all knowledge. Actually, the life of faith is a process of gaining wisdom. "If any of you lacks wisdom," James advised, "he should ask God, who gives generously to all without finding fault, and it will be given to him" (James 1:5). Once prayer moves upward to God, belief must sit at the wheel, and doubt must take the back seat. "When he asks," James continued, "he must believe and not doubt" (1:6). Honest praying is the antidote to honest doubting.

The doubting life fades into the faithful life one

question at a time. Prayer leads to wisdom; wisdom plants the seed of persuasion; persuasion ripens into faith; and faith becomes a passionate habit of life.

30
The Fulfilled Life

It is written, man does not live by bread alone."
There is a hunger deep within the soul that quests
after things which are spiritual. This is no mere
religious whim, no vague transient emotion. It is a
basic need of humanity. "All man's efforts are for his
mouth," wrote Solomon, "yet his appetite is never
satisfied" (Eccles. 6:7).

David experienced this spiritual yearning and wrote,
"As the deer pants for streams of water, so my soul
pants for you, O God. My soul thirsts for God, for the
living God" (Ps. 42:1). While in the desert of Judah, the
psalmist described the parched condition of his soul:

> O God, you are my God,
>   earnestly I seek you;
> My soul thirsts for you,
>   my body longs for you,
> In a dry and weary land
>   where there is no water.
>   (Ps. 63:1)

The search for personal fulfillment is threaded
throughout the Bible. It is no isolated theme. In the
moving dialogue between two lovers in the Song of

Solomon we hear the cry of the beloved: "I looked for the one my heart loves; I looked for him but did not find him" (3:1).

The prophets knew something of the cry of the soul. Isaiah warned of false faith in mediums and spiritualists. Those who seek answers by consulting the dead will roam the land distressed and hungry, he warned. "When they are famished, they will become enraged and, looking upward, will curse their king and their God" (Isa. 8:21).

In blunt, direct fashion the weeping prophet Jeremiah included the word of Jehovah: "My people have committed two sins: they have forsaken me, the spring of living water, and have dug their own cisterns, broken cisterns that cannot hold water" (2:13).

Those who seat themselves well at the table of life while leaving God outside the door invite the greatest poverty. Jesus warned, "Woe to you who are well fed now, for you will go hungry" (Luke 6:25).

Despite the daily struggles to survive, it is better to serve God than eat bread. Our temptation is to hoard to ourselves the material things of life, hoping to gain ultimate security. Jesus taught us simply to pray. "Give us each day our daily bread" (Luke 11:3).

When our higher needs assert themselves there is only one source of fulfillment. God alone can satisfy the longings of the soul.

Denial of the spiritual dimension to life produces its own kind of lunacy. "I have seen another evil under the sun," wrote Solomon. "God gives a man wealth, possessions and honor, so that he lacks nothing his heart desires, but God does not enable him to enjoy them" (Eccles. 6:1, 2). Better to have an ounce of tranquility than a pound of labor chasing after the wind.

Those who seek personal fulfillment in this life only are in for disappointment. "The world and its desires pass away," wrote John the Evangel, "but the man who does the will of God lives forever" (1 John 2:17).

One spiritual truth wholeheartedly believed is worth more than the whole of a religious creed. In the words, "Man shall not live by bread alone, but by every word that proceeds from the mouth of God" (Matt. 4:4, RSV), we have pierced the deep well of God's measureless truth and are satisfied.

31
The Good Life

Mark Twain, the great American humorist, once quipped, "Do good and you become lonesome." While doing good is mocked by cynics, its healing touch changes our world. Doing good, in reality, makes sense. The lonesome doer, in the end, just might become a majority of one.

The "good life" is usually thought to be a life in the fast lane, a materially posh and pleasant life.

Advertisements cater to the tastes of people who worry about image. Reflecting the craze for creating an image of success, some bold messages appear in public. A cereal company boasts, "You know when you have it good," and a cigarette company claims that its product is "the taste of success." A leading business journal reports the prevailing mood of Yuppies: "I deserve to pamper myself."

Where in all of this insanity is the desire to fulfill the higher instincts of humanity? Where is the Christian ideal of service above self? The open ambition and flounting of elitist tastes are not traits consistent with the simple teaching of Jesus, who went about doing good. "Who is wise . . . among you?" asked James. "Let him show it by his good life, by deeds done in the humility that comes from wisdom" (James 3:13).

The quest for the good life is a false substitute for the life of faith. Jesus taught that we should not lay up treasures on earth which are easily destroyed. Rather, he set forth an enduring principle, one that was good for individuals and for society. "The good man," he advised, "brings good things out of the good stored up in his heart" (Luke 6:45).

If the good life is really a life characterized as selflessness and service, where then should we begin? The Bible makes it perfectly clear that mankind is not inherently good. "There is not a righteous man on earth who does what is right and never sins," concluded Solomon (Eccles. 7:20). The indictment is even harsher by David the psalmist: "There is no one who does good" (Ps. 14:1).

We must begin by admitting the absolute bankruptcy of the human soul. Only God's offer of grace and goodness can make us whole and capable of living a consistent life of selflessness.

Goodness is a gift, a fruit of the spirit. Only a few times in the New Testament is the word *goodness* used. In each instance it means doing good to others. "Live as children of the light," Paul urged. "The fruit of the light consists in all goodness, righteousness and truth" (Eph. 5:9).

The secret of the good life is bound up in one of the apostle Paul's prayers: "We constantly pray for you, that our God may count you worthy of his calling, and that by his power he may fulfill every good purpose of yours and every act prompted by your faith" (2 Thess. 1:11). That is it! Every act is to be prompted by faith. Only then does it qualify as a good deed.

Does this mean that all the philanthropy and

good works of well-meaning people are worthless? Not at all. Our world would be a miserable place were it not for the goodness of friend and neighbor and parent. All of these are the result of God's shower of grace and providence on all mankind. However, saving grace not only equips one for heaven; it also fits one best for this life. Out of gratitude to this gracious God we then do good to all, as the Bible instructs.

The good life is rooted in the nature of God himself. It takes its pattern from Jesus, and flows from the transformed inner life of the spirit.

Take the lead in doing good. Others may follow, but even if they don't, you can be sure of good reward.

32
The Honest Life

Honesty is always the best policy. As a maxim it has few equals. George Washington included these words in his farewell address in 1796, and Cervantes's famous character Don Quixote spoke them in the seventeenth-century novel by the same name. But it is the Bible that elevates this lofty principle to prominence. It towers like an Everest over lesser virtues.

Honesty leads the list in the Philippian letter of the seven cardinal virtues of the Christian experience (4:8). However, many people live at another level, choosing a kind of expedient behavior; whatever works for personal gain sets the norm for their actions. Honesty is a good policy only if there is the possibility of getting caught in a dishonest act.

In contrast, the apostle Paul set a standard of impeccable honesty. "We have renounced secret and shameful ways," he said. "We do not use deception" (2 Cor. 4:2). To the Christians in Rome he wrote, "Be careful to do what is right in the eyes of everybody" (Rom. 12:17).

Honesty is even good psychology. The father of modern psychoanalytic theory, Sigmund Freud, advised: "Being entirely honest with oneself is a good exercise." There is a malady of the mind which produces systematic deception. It leaves its wrecks by the side of the road.

Politicians and militarists have lauded the virtue of honesty. Oliver Cromwell, at the height of England's civil war, proclaimed, "A few honest men are better than numbers." He had learned his lesson well from the Bible. Who can ignore the effectiveness of Gideon's three hundred fighting men? Or who can fault the apostles for insisting on honesty as the fundamental trait of deacons?

Honesty is more than a story about George Washington cutting down a cherry tree. It is bedrock Christianity at work. It is the stuff that good marriages are made of, the unwritten trust of all legal contracts. A person's word should be as good as a signature on a document.

When all is said and done more is said than done, as the saying goes. The steady, consistent, faithful word followed by deeds marks the superior person.

Whether we stumble or fall, we must think only of rising again and going on. Our faults, even the fault of dishonesty, can be forgiven. Once cured of vain confidence in ourselves, François Fénelon once observed, we can progress in the spiritual experience.

In our search for wisdom we sift out truth from error, the better from the best. God meets us at the end of our quest and reveals himself as the Father of Lights who does not change like shifting shadows. He is a reliable God.

"I should like to speak of God not on the borders of life but at its center," wrote Dietrich Bonhoeffer from a Nazi prison. "Not in man's suffering and death but in his life and prosperity." Honesty clothes the common habits of daily living more than a martyr's cross. It is a virtue on public display every day.

We need not practice heroics, only plain, simple honesty.

33

The Restrained Life

Patient restraint ranks high as a fundamental quality of living. To be temperate in taste, moderate in manner, and reserved in judgment is to display marks of a superior person. One of the proverbs states that a person who lacks self-control is like a city whose walls are broken down.

The ideal of restraint has been around a long time. The ancient Chinese believed that the firm, the enduring, the simple, and the modest are near to virtue. Moderation was held in high regard by the Greeks. But the Bible states the truth more directly: "Let your moderation be known unto all men" (Phil. 4:5, KJV).

What is true in the spirit is also true in society. Daniel Webster once wrote, "Liberty exists in proportion to restraint." To lose restraint is counterproductive to both inner tranquility and peaceful relations with others.

Imagine unbridled, freewheeling, unrestrained living. A trail of destruction is left in its wake. Personal liberty without accompanying responsibility towards others is harmful. Life has its odd twist. Ultimately the one who presses freedom to excess becomes the victim. Passionate desire beyond the boundaries of propriety eats like a canker in the soul.

The Preacher (Eccles. 1:1, RSV) knew this. Putting the search for pleasure to the test, Solomon came to the following conclusion:

> I denied myself nothing my eyes desired:
>   I refused my heart no pleasure.
> My heart took delight in all my work,
>   And this was the reward for all my labor.
> Yet when I surveyed all that my hands had done
>   And what I had toiled to achieve,
> Everything was meaningless, a chasing after the
>   wind;
>   Nothing was gained under the sun.
>
> (Eccles. 2:10–11)

Contentment is a gift. Those who have insatiable appetites, who are always desiring more of things or of others, are never fully satisfied. Bernard of Clairvaux discovered this principle in the eleventh century. "We want to satisfy all our desires," he wrote, "and find we cannot get possession of all things." It is nature's law, it seems, that makes us place higher value on what we don't have. We begin to loathe what we have and in restless abandon long for things not ours.

Restraint is the antidote to sinful cravings. The age-old law of the seed and the sower returns time and time again to haunt us. "Do not be deceived," wrote Paul to Galatian Christians. "God cannot be mocked. A man reaps what he sows. The one who sows to please his sinful nature, from that nature will reap destruction" (Gal. 6:7–8). On the other

105

hand, "the one who sows to please the Spirit" will reap life everlasting.

There are those whose motto is, "Do what comes naturally." The slow, inexorable, downward path to destruction is certain unless God and his laws are accounted for. Let love be your aim. Such a rule becomes golden. When its healing pattern sets a direction toward positive relationships with God and others, peace is the product.

We can destroy ourselves by lack of restraint. It doesn't even take the devil to do it. Merely preventing the activity of the Spirit by showing fits of temper and bitterness corrupts the soul. "Do not give the devil a foothold" (Eph. 4:27), the Bible warns; the instruction to "get rid of all bitterness, rage and anger" (:31) is good advice as well.

We can also miss the grace of God by lack of restraint. When a root of bitterness springs up in the soul it troubles the calm waters of inner peacefulness and defiles many (Heb. 12:15).

Life in the Spirit gives us the moral armament to reverse the natural impulses of sexual immorality, hatred, discord, jealousy, rage, dissent, envy, drunkenness, and the like. Each of these unrestrained reactions carry the warning, "those who practice such things shall not inherit the kingdom of God" (Gal. 5:21, NASB).

Character is much easier kept than recovered. In the end the restrained person is the winner. When we moderate our passions, control our tempers, and direct our energies toward loving God and others we enter the peaceable kingdom of inner tranquility and outward harmony.

34
The Suffering Life

It should come as no surprise to Christians that suffering comes with discipleship. Jesus predicted it and even pronounced his blessing upon it: "Blessed are you when people insult you, persecute you and falsely say all kinds of evil against you because of me" (Matt. 5:11).

The Christian doctrine of suffering explains a curious fact about our world, according to C. S. Lewis in *The Problem of Pain*. The settled peace and security which we all desire are elusive. At the same time, our lives are sprinkled with joy, pleasure, and merriment. "We are never safe," Lewis wrote, "but we have plenty of fun, and some ecstasy."

Make no mistake. Happy moments of love, a sunset, a concert, shared years with family—these are exceptions. We dare not mistake these for heaven and home. We are pilgrims passing through, strangers in a foreign land. Suffering is part of the turf.

The curse, we say, started it all. Had Adam and Eve not sinned in the garden, all would be well. It doesn't help to speculate, however. We can curse the curse but it does no good. Thorns and thistles are here to stay until the day of final redemption.

This does not mean that we merely accommodate ourselves to evil. Quite the contrary. It is better, someone has said, to light a candle than curse the darkness. The beautiful thing about our world is that God lit that first candle. Light has shined in on this world through Jesus who was and is the Light of the World. Because Jesus conquered death and spiritual darkness we have a chance of taking our suffering in stride. The curse has been forever blunted by the cross, and suffering takes on a new dimension.

While every citizen of the heavenly kingdom walks a weary road on earth, we need not walk alone. Jesus suffered, leaving us an example. He didn't sin and no deceit was found in his mouth. When they hurled insults, he did not retaliate; when he suffered, he made no threats.

This is no grin-and-bear-it style. The stiff upper lip has no place in Christian suffering. Jesus showed us how to suffer, as the apostle Peter reported: "He entrusted himself to (God) who judges justly" (1 Peter 2:23).

No part of us craves persecution. But it will come. For those spared the trials of outright hostile attack for their faith in Christ, there comes, nevertheless, that slow, certain travail that accompanies our humanity. There is no exemption clause inserted in the contract of life just because we are Christians. Even the physical world around us has been "groaning as in the pains of childbirth right up to the present time" (Rom. 8:22).

There is a divine purpose that shines through suffering, as light filters through a dark curtain. As a fellow sufferer, I claim no clairvoyance or mystical answer to an old mystery. Yet God is filling his world with glory. Even the heavens are telling it (Ps. 19).

What is this glory? The prophets predicted the sufferings of Jesus and the glories that should follow. Even the creation waits eagerly for the final revelation. Glory is the unveiling of God's nature. Here we see through a glass dimly. But someday, when we stand face to face with God our judge his glory will be revealed.

All of this means that suffering is a temporary discomfort. I do not mean to demean it or to minimize it. Those who suffer know its terror. But the terror is temporary and brief compared to eternity. "We suffer only once," wrote Sören Kierkegaard, "but we triumph eternally."

Let us try to gain a truer view of where we are in relation to the fall of Adam. The current depravity, whether it manifests itself in pain, sorrow, sin, or even death, has met its match at Golgotha. Now we await the final redemption. "Rejoice and be glad, because great is your reward in heaven" (Matt. 5:12).

35
The Convinced Life

Becoming a convinced Christian is not the result of buying a "sales pitch." Mature saints are not the product of a marketing strategy. They are the superb handiwork of God. This is what is meant by Christians being the workmanship of God created in Christ Jesus unto good works.

The convinced life grows from deep faith in God. Shallow faith wears thin over the long haul. "Deep calleth unto deep," sang the psalmist (Ps. 42:7, KJV). The interior power of faith flows upward and outward from deep springs of the soul.

Integrity marks the convinced life. Interior faith differs from hypocritical external faith. Jesus knew this when he indicted the Pharisees with the terse charge, "They say things but do not do them (Matt. 23:3, NASB).

A life of integrity has the same quality inside and out. We can be fooled by appearances, even when assessing ourselves. Only God knows what is at the core of a life. "The Lord does not look at the things man looks at. Man looks at the outward appearance, but the LORD looks at the heart" (1 Sam. 16:7).

The building of an inner faith in God is like building a carefully crafted house. One doesn't begin with the external landscaping. First, the foundation, then the framing. Christian educator Henrietta Mears used to say that skyscrapers aren't built from the top down.

It is the same way with our lives. "No one can lay any foundation other than the one already laid, which is Jesus Christ" (1 Cor. 3:11). Lives built on wood, hay, and stubble—and even gold, silver, and costly stones—don't last. Christ must never be merely on the borders of our lives but at the center.

The convinced life is motivated from within. This inner-directed life is similar to an artesian well. Like pressure from subterranean reservoirs, the Christ-life bubbles up, refreshing both the soul and society.

Few of us operate this way. We become other-directed, worrying too much what others will think of us. This chokes the free, open spirit of faithfulness to God. People pull the strings of our lives but God demands absolute lordship.

"We are all equal in sin and in moral wretchedness," wrote Paul Tournier. We can take pride in detailing our successes, we can even claim to know the secret of happiness and excellence. Such reassurances gloss over the festering inner problems of greed, lust, impatience, and the absence of love. God wants to forgive us of these deceptions.

A person may be a religious unbeliever. Einstein felt he fit that description and claimed such in a letter to a friend, writing, "I am a deeply religious unbeliever." By contrast, the convinced life is based on the only sure solution to the sin question. Burdens really are lifted at Calvary. Guilt vanishes when the blood of Christ is applied to sin.

A woman going through the agony of divorce

confided that her life contained a great deal of pain. She openly professed faith and confessed her sin. After turning to Christ she told others that a great burden had been lifted.

Such is the happy prospect of all who become convinced followers of Jesus. "Christian experience," Paul Tournier wrote in *Escape from Loneliness*, "first of all restores the human person and spreads out from person to person until it transforms society." Delivered from the chains of our own imprisonment, we experience the fresh winds of grace, and others share its calming effect.

The convinced life is worthless until it converts itself into conduct. You call yourself a Christian? Then let your life match your ideals.

36
The Merciful Life

The Bible tells us to do some impossible things, like showing mercy. Jesus said, "Be merciful, just as your Father is merciful" (Luke 6:36). That is a high order and one trait which does not come easily for most of us.

Mercy is a quality God possesses. Moses encountered it on Mount Sinai: "The LORD, the LORD, a God merciful and gracious, slow to anger, and abounding in steadfast love and faithfulness" (Exod. 34:6, RSV). While an attribute of God, it is a quality he shares uniquely with us.

Thought by many to be a sign of weakness, mercy has long been a missing commodity in this world. It's lack was apparent in Old Testament times, for prophets like Hosea thundered, "Keep mercy and judgment" (Hos. 12:6, KJV); and Jeremiah warned Israel of coming captors, "They are cruel and show no mercy" (Jer. 6:23).

It is the cry of penitent sinners ("God be merciful" —Luke 18:13) and the perfection of the saints ("Blessed are the merciful"—Matt. 5:7). Among first-century Christians mercy was a common form of greeting in letters, and from 250 B.C. onward the word signified alms or gifts to the poor. Paul lists mercy among the gifts of the Holy Spirit given to the church (Rom. 12:8).

The Bible teaches that mercy is the wellspring of redemption. God, who is rich in mercy (Eph. 2:4), saved us from our sins (Titus 3:5). He contrived not our ruin, but our recovery.

All true service in Jesus' name is prompted by mercy. It was on this basis that Paul appealed to Roman Christians to present themselves as living sacrifices to God (Rom. 12:1). Mercy is something we are to put on, like an article of clothing (Col. 3:12). The misery of our world needs the mercy of God ministered by servants of God.

Nowhere is this more clear than in the teaching of Jesus about inheriting the kingdom:

> I was hungry and you gave me food;
> I was thirsty and you gave me drink;
> I was a stranger and you welcomed me;
> I was naked and you clothed me;
> I was sick and you visited me;
> I was in prison and you came to me.
> (Matt. 25:35–36, RSV)

To ignore these compassions, Jesus taught, is to miss an incalculable inheritance.

Mercy is one word that cries out for tangible expression. A living example of this virtue is worth far more than words. Following the Second World War, several young German women banded together to engage in acts of mercy. With Sister Basilea Shlink at their head, they sought to demonstrate repentance for the crimes of the German people against the Jews and the human race. Their sole mission was to engage in acts of compassion and mercy. In these *Evangelical Sisters of Mercy* we have living proof that mercy is alive and well in a merciless society.

It was D. L. Moody who said, "A Christian is the world's Bible and some need revising." If the pure, simple virtue of mercy is to touch the hurts of our world, it is up to us. Mercy reverses the vengeful act and unforgiving spirit. It bends down to lift up the fallen, encourage the rebellious, and lead the lost.

On February 12, 1883, Charles Hadden Spurgeon, then England's leading preacher, delivered a sermon based on the text of Hosea 2:23, "I will have mercy upon her that had not obtained mercy" (KJV). He warned Englanders that without mercy there could be no approval from God, no good thing from God, no application of Christ's blood, no saving work of the Holy Spirit, no fellowship, and no hope of heaven. How quaint, we say one hundred years later, to think that a preacher would arouse sleepy nineteenth-century Christians with the soft and tender word of mercy.

At the point in time when the whole world comes crashing down around us, we may need the kind of prayer Paul once prayed for a troubled man: "The LORD grant unto him that he may find mercy of the LORD in that day" (2 Tim. 1:18, KJV).

I, for one, want to be an agent of mercy.

37
The Joyful Life

One quality of life stands out as the mood most likely to succeed. Its effect on us is like strong medicine, and when others see it in us they find healing for their souls as well. That one quality is joy.

No word is more misunderstood than this word *joy*. Usually people want to equate it with happiness, but such cannot be done. Happiness, pursued by all and even guaranteed in the Declaration of Independence, is a surface emotion, transient, fickle, sure to fade under life's pressures. Joy is for the long haul. It is an inner emotion, bedrock psychological substance.

We live in a quick-fix society. Moods are easily altered, even controlled, by drugs and other mind-manipulating substances. But there is more to life than preoccupation with shaping moods, with concocting happiness all the time. Life is not an escalator on which one jumps when desiring to go either up or down.

Joy is one of the emotions close to the core of the human soul. It is a fruit of the Holy Spirit (Gal. 5:22). It cannot be pumped up, tacked on, or cheered into existence by some well-meaning friend who is merely interested in our sense of well-being. It is triggered in our hearts in response to God's great gift of love and forgiveness. It is simply what the Bible says it is—a gift.

The word itself appears in the Scriptures in surprising fashion. One might expect it to be celebrative—and it is. The Psalms exude the festal aspect of joy: "Rejoice in the LORD" (Ps. 33:1, KJV); "O Come, let us sing unto the LORD: let us make a joyful noise to the rock of our salvation" (Ps. 95:1, KJV). Joy is linked to our eternal destiny, glory itself.

In quite another connection, the word *joy* appears paradoxically with suffering, trials, and tribulation. Thus, it is more than mood. Jesus taught that sorrow, even the kind prompted by persecution, would turn to joy (John 16:20). James outlandishly urged Christians to "count it all joy" (1:2, RSV) when facing trials. In similar fashion, Peter, whose brush with trouble was legendary, painted a picture of pure joy in the midst of suffering (1 Peter 1:6).

How can this be? How can a person rejoice in trouble? The answer to this seeming paradox lies in the nature of our identification with Jesus Christ. The startling fact that Jesus set the pattern of joy by enduring the cross (Heb. 12:2) forever casts "joy" into a different light than most moderns view it.

In his essay titled, "We Have No Right to Happiness," C. S. Lewis dug deeply into the rich soil of faith to explain the nature of Christian joy. "A right to happiness doesn't, for me, make more sense than a right to be six feet tall, or to have a millionaire for your father, or to get good weather whenever you want to have a picnic," he wrote. Joy is what we are surprised at. It is deep-seated satisfaction, a gift of the indwelling Spirit.

Joy rides through tough times. Like the memory of a pleasant moment, it recurs in the heart as a sought-after, steady diet.

When one discovers joy, the false substitutes pale into insignificance. Psychological kicks have their moment in the sun, but turn ashen grey with time. Our civilization will have died at heart when joy is ever replaced by surface mood, or transient emotion.

The ancient Greek philosophers contemplated this emotion. Like people in our day, they substituted the word *pleasure* for joy, but Christians recovered the term. The kingdom of God, Paul taught, "is not meat and drink; but righteousness, and peace, and joy..." (Rom. 14:17, KJV).

Joy, then, is that inner satisfaction that all is well with the soul, destiny is assured, and the troubles of life are only passing irritants. Joy can become for all of us the source of song, the focal point of hope, and the fuel for lasting satisfaction and true happiness.

38
The Meaningful Life

The meaning of life is to build a life as if it were a work of art. Admittedly this poses a problem. What is art to one is junk to another. Such is the sad state of affairs when it comes to both character and taste.

Like all good art, life should reveal a design. Random lines and careless squibs themselves do not make for good art. Neither does a directionless life make for good character.

Simplicity is the true soul of art. It also forms the core of character. At bedrock the Christian life is the Christ-life. To live is Christ, according to the apostle Paul. It was for this high purpose that God took on human form—to make himself visible and understood in simple terms.

"I am come that (you) might have life," announced Jesus (John 10:10, KJV). In his coming and in his caring Jesus demonstrated what real life was all about.

"Be careful how you build," is sound advice for life. The unwise build on the shifting and unstable sands of unbelief and uncertainty. The wise erect a life on the firm foundation of faith and certainty.

It is not easy to build a life full of character. Nor does it happen in a moment, like mixing instant coffee in hot water. Character is the ability to carry out a right choice long after the emotion of making the decision has passed. Choice, however, is where it all begins.

"Choose life," cried Moses in the wilderness (Deut. 30:19). This implies that there are other choices one could make, other turns in the road. "Follow me," Jesus invites. Our freedom allows us to decide not to follow, but it does not allow us to decide to be undecided. "How long will you waver between two opinions?" Elijah asked the wavering citizens of an eighth-century B.C. world. "If the LORD is God, follow him" (1 Kings 18:21). The same choice is ours today. We cannot stand long in the valley of indecision.

Winston Churchill once referred to his opponents in the British Parliament as those who were "decided only to be undecided, resolved to be irresolute, adamant for drift, solid for fluidity, all-powerful to be impotent." Some people are like that.

Christ invites us to discover the meaning of life and to experience it to the fullest. He asks us to bare our secret faults and to understand the immensity of God's forgiveness.

The most wonderful thing in this world is not the good that we accomplish, but the good that God has done on our behalf. Jesus came to call sinners to repentance, not good people to get their acts together. Divine grace means just what the line of the hymn says: "He saw me plunged in deep despair and flew to my relief."

Life is an incredible journey. Along that journey are a myriad of choices, the sum of which shape our destiny.

"We are always wanting to change institutions, and to change other people," observed Swiss psychiatrist Paul Tournier in *Person Reborn.* "The Spirit brings us back to our own need of inner change."

In this we are not left alone. God's Spirit shapes us, re-creates us into a new image—the image of Christ (2 Cor. 5:17). This is no plastic deity at work. The same God who shaped our incredibly beautiful universe shapes our souls. Like a mist that is cleared by sunshine, the soul that turns to God enters the bright sunlight of life.

The art of living is not framed canvas or pedestaled statuary. It is the vibrant recovery of a lost creation. Ultimately the meaning of life is found in re-establishing the relationship with God that was originally intended in creation. Faith in Christ opens the door to the meaningful life.

39
The Sorrowful Life

Grief and sorrow touch every person's life. They are part and parcel of our humanity. All that is this side of Eden and short of heaven is imperfect. Mortality is written all over our short span of life.

These tragic twins show no favoritism. Grief and sorrow are the lot of saint and sinner alike. "Many are the sorrows of the wicked," wrote the psalmist (32:10, NASB) and the preacher said of mankind, "All his days his task is painful and grievous (Eccles. 2:23, NASB). Even our perfect Savior, the Lord himself, was a "man of sorrows...acquainted with grief" (Isa. 53:3, KJV).

Like many deep truths, sorrow and grief are paradoxical. That is to say that they are to be preferred over the ruin of a wasted life. Solomon wrote, "Sorrow is better than laughter, for by a sad countenance the heart is made better."

There is a type of sorrow which turns life for the better. Paul spoke of it in relation to repentance. "Godly sorrow," he told Corinthian Christians, "brings repentance" (2 Cor. 7:10).

Poets and hymn writers in the past have known the dimensions of sorrow and grief. These are the stuff of life, to be borne triumphantly. Sorrows were like billowing seas to Horatio G. Spafford and an apt description of all of life to the Danish hymnist, Baring-Gould. His lines, "Through the night of doubt and sorrow, onward goes the pilgrim band," have inspired generations to look toward the promised land ahead. John Newton, the converted slave trader, spoke of the sweet sound of Jesus' name which "soothes his sorrows, heals his wounds and drives away his fears."

While trouble is certain, God's sheltering care is more certain still. Who has not longed for the arms of Jesus? "He shall cover thee with his feathers," the psalmist said, describing God's care, "and under his wings shalt thou trust" (Ps. 91:4, KJV).

"Keep close to Jesus in life and in death," advised Thomas à Kempis, "and commit yourself into His faithfulness, who, when all fail, can alone help you." Such wisdom is rare. Its soothing touch is like the legendary balm of Gilead, an ointment rendered from trees in ancient Jordan. "There is a balm in Gilead," goes the Negro spiritual, "that heals the wounded soul."

We are never alone in our sorrows. Jesus is by our side. The shortest verse in the Bible, John 11:35, bears eloquent testimony to the truth that Jesus cares. History's perfect and complete Man stood by a grave and cried.

God cares for us at all times. He never goes off duty and, as Psalm 121 tells us, never slumbers or sleeps.

Those who know God and have built a long acquaintance with his Word reap a rich harvest when grief and sorrow pay their visit. While the pain is sharp and real, the presence of God heals our hurts and mends our brokenness. God comforts the downcast (2 Cor. 7:6).

We all long for an escape from a sorrowful life. A pastor friend, whose young son died in the prime of his youth, described the agony and the accompanying answer to his heart's cry.

> In the darkest year of my life when I cried until I could cry no more, I could still rejoice because my joy was not based on my feelings.

The story is told of actress Helen Hayes, who, upon the death of her daughter became deeply despondent. "I couldn't order faith the way you order a good dinner," she wrote years later. Then, however, she reached out in the manner discussed in Psalm 40: "I waited patiently for the Lord; and he inclined unto me, and heard my cry" (v. 1, KJV).

That is how our great God touches our grief and soothes our sorrows.

40

The Successful Life

The passion to succeed burns within all of us. From childhood onward, we are prodded along the road of life by anxious parents, teachers, and well-meaning relatives. Unless this passion is snuffed out by ridicule, accumulated failures, or despair, the quest to make it in life drives us onward.

The fear of failure, however, haunts many people. Like a towering mountain, the fear of not succeeding stands as an obstacle to success. For some, it even holds them back from trying. Many of them give up too early. It is just too difficult to climb that mountain—and to remove it seems out of the question.

We must beware of success as a goal in life. It is like a fire in an oil refinery. Difficult to extinguish once ignited, the quest for success consumes with unrelenting fury. (This does not mean that we should ignore ambition. The absence of drive and aspiration can be equally as destructive as the burning passion to succeed.)

Success isn't what most of us think it to be. There are a lot of false definitions around. Take fame and fortune, for example. Can success be found in fame? In chapter 20 of the Gospel of Matthew, Jesus warned against seeking prominence

(v. 25, 26). Fame is a false goal. Those who achieve it are usually not the same ones who seek it. Even the ones who arrive at the top find it an uneasy perch. They are easily toppled and soon forgotten.

Jesus also warned against laying up treasures on earth (Matt. 6:19). There is wisdom in this. For one thing, wealth is illusory; we cannot obtain in this life all that we desire. No one ever has enough without wanting more. The poor have despaired of ever accumulating it and the wealthy are rarely satisfied by having it. As a measure of success, then, money too is a poor indicator.

If success is not what most define it to be, then what is it? The real issue is discovering the focus of life's energies, choosing proper goals. In the Old Testament, success was tied to obedience to the law of God. "Do not let this Book of the Law depart from your mouth; meditate on it day and night, so that you may be careful to do everything written in it. Then you will be prosperous and successful" (Josh. 1:8).

In the New Testament, Jesus gave us the clue to success in the Beatitudes. The power of these incredible statements lies in their reversal of human values. What counts with God is fidelity, simple pity, purity of heart, and unselfish readiness to assist the cause of peace.

Try reading each beatitude using the word *successful* instead of *blessed* and you will uncover the tip of a great treasure. It will then take a lifetime to discover the full-orbed meaning of true success.

A modern version of the beatitudes might read like this:

Blessed are the proud, for theirs is the accumulation of power and influence.

Blessed are those with the "stiff upper lip," for they shall stick things out through thick and thin.

Blessed are the pushy, for they have their reward.

Blessed are those who hunger and thirst after evil, for they shall have to be satisfied with what they get.

Blessed are the vindictive and spiteful, for they shall receive the same.

Blessed are the pornography peddlers, for they won't have a ghost of a chance of seeing God.

Blessed are the fighters and rioters, for they shall be called the sons of war.

When we reflect on what success in life really is, we are strangely drawn to Christ and his teachings. When we see the genuine thing, the fake and phony pale into insignificance.

Moved by the enduring truths of the Bible, English journalist Malcomb Muggeridge once wrote: "Civilizations die. Our Lord cannot die and I have come to feel that the only things that I consider utterly and pledge myself to are things that are eternal."

The successful life, in the proper coinage of the Christian experience, means living up to the high ideals of the transformed life in Christ.